KU-773-275

A Scolar Press Facsimile

SILEX SCINTILLANS

Henry Vaughan

1650

EDINBURGH UNIVERSITY LIBRARY

WITHDRAWN

Printed and published in Great Britain by
The Scolar Press Limited, Menston, Yorkshire
and 39 Great Russell Street, London WC1

This facsimile first published 1968
Reprinted 1973

ISBN

0 85417 710 8

Cloth

ISBN

0 85417 709 4

Paper

Introductory Note

Reproduced (original size) by permission of the Trustees of the British Museum. Shelf-mark: 238.b.8.

Henry Vaughan, self-styled 'Silurist' because his home county of Breconshire was once inhabited by the Silures, was born in 1622, entered Jesus College, Oxford, in 1638, studied law for a short while in London, but eventually devoted his life to medicine, practising in Newton-by-Usk from 1650 until his death in 1695.

Vaughan's first volume of poetry appeared in 1646 with the title *Poems, with the tenth Satyre of Juvenal Englished*. *Olor Iscanus*, consisting of some original poetry and translations, appeared in 1651. The last poetical collection published in his lifetime was *Thalia rediviva* (1678). His prose works were translations of Latin: *The Mount of Olives*, 1652 (by Anselm); *Flores Solitudinis*, 1654 (from works by Nierembergius and Eucherius); *Hermetical physic*, 1655, and *The Chemist's Key*, 1657, both by Henricus Nollius. There is no doubt, however, that his fame rests squarely on *Silex Scintillans* ('sparkling flint') first published in 1650, and reprinted in 1655 with the addition of a second collection of poems, including the celebrated 'They are all gone into the world of light', 'The Bird', 'The Waterfall', and 'Quicknesse'.

Vaughan's poetry enjoyed little popularity during his lifetime, and less in the hundred and fifty odd years which elapsed before the Chiswick Press reprint of *Silex Scintillans* by H. F. Lyte in 1847. Real recognition of his genius did not come until the appearance in 1868 of A. B. Grosart's edition in four volumes of the *Works in Verse and Prose*. The standard edition is still that of L. C. Martin (Oxford, 1957).

Of the many studies, biographical and critical, devoted to Vaughan the following are important: F. E. Hutchinson, *Henry Vaughan* (1947); E. Blunden, *On the Poems of Henry Vaughan* (1927); T. S. Eliot's essay in *The Dial* (Vol. 73, 1927); R. Garner, *Henry Vaughan* (1959); and E. C. Pettet, *Of Paradise and Light* (1960). For a bibliography see E. L. Marilla, *A Comprehensive Bibliography of Henry Vaughan* (University of Alabama, 1948).

Reference: Wing V 125.

Authoris (de se) Emblema.

T Entásti, fateor, sine vulnere sæpius, & me
  Consultũ voluit Vox, sine voce, frequens,
Ambivit placido divinior aura meatu,
  Et frustrà sancto murmure præmonuit
Surdus eram, mutusq; Silex: Tu (quanta tuorum
  Cura tibi est!) aliâ das renovare viâ,
Permutas Curam: Jamq; irritatus Amorem
  Posse negas, & vim, Vi, superare paras,
Accedis proptor, molemq;, & Saxea rumpis
  Pectora, sitq; Caro, quod fuit ante Lapis
En lacerum! Cælosq; tuos ardentia tandem
  Fragmenta, & liquidas ex Adamante genæ.
Sic olim urdantes Petras, Scopulosq; vomentes
  Curásti, O populi providus usq; tui!
Quam miranda tibi manus est! Moriendo, revixi;
  Et fractas jam sum ditior inter opes.

Silex Scintillans:
or
SACRED POEMS
and
Private Eiaculations
By
Henry Vaughan *Silurist* K

LONDON *Printed by T.W. for H.Blunden* at *ỹ Castle in Cornehill*. 1650

The Dedication.

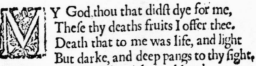

MY God, thou that didſt dye for me,
These thy deaths fruits I offer thee.
Death that to me was life, and light
But darke, and deep pangs to thy ſight,
Some drops of thy all-quickning bloud
Fell on my heart, theſe made it bud
And put forth thus, though, Lord, before
The ground was curs'd, and void of ſtore.
  Indeed, I had ſome here to hire
Which long reſiſted thy deſire,
That ſton'd thy Servants, and did move
To have thee murther'd for thy Love,
But, Lord, I have expell'd them, and ſo bent
Begge thou wouldſt take thy Tenants Rent.

Silex Scintillans, &c.

Regeneration.

AWard, and still in bonds, one day
     I stole abroad,
It was high-spring, and all the way
    Primros'd, and hung with shade ;
     Yet, was it frost within,
      And surly winds
Blasted my infant buds, and sinne
     Like Clouds ecclips'd my mind.

2.

Storm'd thus ; I straight perceiv'd my spring
     Meere stage, and show,
My walke a monstrous, mountain'd thing
    Rough-cast with Rocks, and snow ;
     And as a Pilgrims Eye
      Far from reliefe,
Measures the melancholy skye
     Then drops, and rains for griefe,

3.

So sigh'd I upwards still, at last
     'Twixt steps, and falls
I reach'd the pinacle, where plac'd
     I found a paire of scales,
     I tooke them up and layd
      In th'one late paines,
The other smoake, and pleasures weigh'd
     But prov'd the heavier graines ;

4.

With that, some cryed, *Away* ; straight I
     Obey'd, and led
Full East, a faire, fresh field could spy
     Some call'd it, *Jacobs Bed* ;

A Virgin-foile, which no
            Rude feet ere trod,
Where (fince he ftept there,) only go
            Prophets, and friends of God.

5.

Here, I repos'd ; but fcarfe well fet,
            A grove defcryed
Of ftately height, whofe branches met
            And mixt on every fide ;
            I entred, and once in
                  (Amaz'd to fee't,)
Found all was chang'd, and a new fpring
            Did all my fenfes greet ;

6.

The unthrift Sunne fhot vitall gold
            A thoufand peeces,
And heaven its azure did unfold
            Checqur'd with fnowie fleeces,
            The aire was all in fpice
                  And every bufh
A garland wore ; Thus fed my Eyes
            But all the Eare lay hufh.

7.

Only a little Fountain lent
            Some ufe for Eares,
And on the dumbe fhades language fpent
            The Mufick of her teares ;
            I drew her neere, and found
                  The Cifterne full
Of divers ftones, fome bright, and round
            Others ill-fhap'd, and dull.

8.

The firft (pray marke,) as quick as light
            Danc'd through the floud,
But, th'laft more heavy then the night
            Nail'd to the Center ftood ;
            I wonder'd much, but tyr'd
                  At laft with thought,
My reftlefs Eye that ftill defir'd
            As ftrange an object brought ;

9.

It was a banke of flowers, where I descried
   (Though 'twas mid-day,)
Some fast asleepe, others broad-eyed
   And taking in the Ray,
   Here musing long, I heard
   A rushing wind
Which still increas'd, but whence it stirr'd
  No where I could not find ;

10.

I turn'd me round, and to each shade
    Dispatch'd an Eye,
To see, if any leafe had made
   Least motion, or Reply,
   But while I listning sought
   My mind to ease
By knowing, where 'twas, or where not,
  It whisper'd; *where I please.*

Lord, then said I, *On me one breath,*
And let me dye before my death!

Cant. Cap. 5. ver. 17.
Arise O North, and come thou South-wind, and blow
upon my garden, that the spices thereof may flow out.

Death.

A Dialogue.

Soule.

'TIs a sad Land, that in one day
  Hath dull'd thee thus, when death shall freeze
Thy bloud to Ice, and thou must stay
Tenant for Yeares, and Centuries,
How wilt thou brook't ? ——

        Body

Body. I cannot tell,——
But if all sence wings not with thee,
And something still be left the dead,
I'le wish my Curtaines off to free
Me from so darke, and sad a bed ;

A neast of nights, a gloomie sphere,
Where shadowes thicken, and the Cloud
Sits on the Suns brow all the yeare,
And nothing moves without a shrowd ;

Soule. 'Tis so : But as thou sawest that night
Wee travell'd in, our first attempts
Were dull, and blind, but Custome straight
Our feares, and falls brought to contempt,

Then, when the gastly *twelve* was past
We breath'd still for a blushing *East*,
And bad the lazie Sunne make hast,
And on sure hopes, though long, did feast ;

But when we saw the Clouds to crack
And in those Cranies light appear'd,
We thought the day then was not slack,
And pleas'd our selves with what wee feard ;

Just so it is in death. But thou
Shalt in thy mothers bosome sleepe
Whilst I each minute grone to know
How neere Redemption creepes.

Then shall wee meet to mixe again, and met,
'Tis last good-night, our Sunne shall never set.

Job, Cap : 10. ver. 21. 22.

Before I goe whence I shall not returne, even to the land of darknesse, and the shadow of death ;

A Land of darknesse, as darkenesse it selfe, and of the shadow of death, without any order, and where the light is as darknesse.

Resurrection

Resurrection and Immortality :

Heb. cap. 10. *ve:* 20.

By that new, and living way, which he hath prepared for us, through the veile, which is his flesh.

Body.

1.

OFt have I seen, when that renewing breath
    That binds, and loosens death
Inspir'd a quickning power through the dead
    Creatures a bed,
    Some drowsie silk-worme creepe
    From that long sleepe
And in weake, infant hummings chime, and knell
    About her silent Cell
Untill at last full with the vitall Ray
    She wing'd away,
    And proud with life, and sence,
    Heav'ns rich Expence,
Esteem'd (vaine things!) of two whole Elements
    As meane, and span-extents.
Shall I then thinke such providence will be
    Lesse friend to me ?
    Or that he can endure to be unjust
Who keeps his Covenant even with our dust?

Soule

Soule.

2.

Poore, querulous handfull! was't for this
        I taught thee all that is ?
Unbowel'd nature, shew'd thee her recruits,
                And Change of suits
        And how of death we make
                A meere mistake,
For no thing can to *Nothing* fall, but still
        Incorporates by skill,
And then returns, and from the wombe of things
                Such treasure brings
        As *Phenix*-like renew'th
                Both life, and youth ;
For a preserving spirit doth still passe
        Untainted through this Masse,
Which doth resolve, produce, and ripen all
                That to it fall ;
        Nor are those births which we
                Thus suffering see
Destroy'd at all ; But when times restles wave
                Their substance doth deprave
And the more noble *Essence* finds his house
                Sickly, and loose,
        He, ever young, doth wing
                Unto that spring,
And *source* of spirits, where he takes his lot
        Till time no more shall rot
His passive Cottage ; which (though laid aside,)
                Like some spruce Bride,
Shall one day rise, and cloath'd with shining light
                All pure, and bright
        Re-marry to the soule, for 'tis most plaine
        Thou only fal'st to be refin'd againe.

3.

Then I that here saw darkly in a glasse
                But mists, and shadows passe,

And

And, by their owne weake *Shine*, did search the springs
             And Course of things
    Shall with Inlightned Rayes
             Peirce all their wayes;
And as thou saw'st, I in a thought could goe
             To Heav'n, or Earth below
To reade some *Starre*, or *Min'rall*, and in State
             There often sate,
    So shalt thou then with me
             (Both wing'd, and free,)
Rove in that mighty, and eternall light
             Where no rude shade, or night
Shall dare approach us ; we shall there no more
             Watch stars, or pore
    Through melancholly clouds, and say
             would it were Day!
One everlasting *Saboth* there shall runne
Without *Succession*, and without a *Sunne*.

Dan : Cap : 12. ver : 13.
*But goe thou thy way untill the end be, for thou shalt rest,
and stand up in thy lot, at the end of the dayes.*

Day of Judgement.

WHen through the North a fire shall rush
             And rowle into the East,
And like a firie torrent brush
             And sweepe up *South*, and *West*,

When all shall streame, and lighten round
             And with surprizing flames
Both stars, and Elements confound
             And quite blot out their names,

When thou shalt spend thy sacred store
             Of thunders in that heate
And low as ere they lay before
             Thy six-dayes-buildings beate,

                    When

When like a scrowle the heavens shal passe
                 And vanish cleane away,
And nought must stand of that vast space
                 Which held up night, and day,

When one lowd blast shall rend the deepe,
                 And from the wombe of earth
Summon up all that are asleepe
                 Unto a second birth,

When thou shalt make the Clouds thy seate,
                 And in the open aire
The Quick, and dead, both small and great
                 Must to thy barre repaire;

O then it wilbe all too late
                 To say, *what shall I doe?*
Repentance there is out of date
                 And so is *mercy* too ;

Prepare, prepare me then, O God !
                 And let me now begin
To feele my loving fathers *Rod*
                 Killing the man of sinne !

Give me, O give me Crosses here,
                 Still more afflictions lend,
That pill, though bitter, is most deare
                 That brings health in the end ;

Lord, God ! I beg nor friends, nor wealth
                 But pray against them both ;
Three things I'de have, my soules chief health!
                 And one of these seme loath,

A living *F A I T H*, a *H E A R T* of flesh,
                 The *W O R L D* an Enemie,
This last will keepe the first two fresh,
                 And bring me, where I'de be.

                                        1 Pet.

. 1 Pet. 4. 7.

Now the end of all things is at hand, be you therefore sober, and watching in prayer.

Religion.

MY God, when I walke in those groves,
  And leaves thy spirit doth still fan,
I see in each shade that there growes
An Angell talking with a man.

Under a *Juniper*, some house,
Or the coole *Mirtles* canopie,
Others beneath an *Oakes* greene boughs,
Or at some *fountaines* bubling Eye ;

Here *Jacob* dreames, and wrestles ; there
Elias by a Raven is fed,
Another time by th' Angell, where
He brings him water with his bread ;

In *Abr'hams* Tent the winged guests
(O how familiar then was heaven !)
Eate, drinke, discourse, sit downe, and rest
Untill the Coole, and shady *Even* ;

Nay thou thy selfe, my God, in *fire*,
whirle-winds, and *Clouds*, and the *soft voice*
Speak'st there so much, that I admire
We have no Conf'rence in these daies ;

Is the truce broke ? or 'cause we have
A mediatour now with thee,
Doest thou therefore old Treaties wave
And by appeales from him decree ?

Or

Or is't so, as some green heads say
That now all miracles must cease?
Though thou hast promis'd they should stay
The tokens of the Church, and peace;

No, no; Religion is a Spring
That from some secret, golden Mine
Derives her birth, and thence doth bring
Cordials in every drop, and Wine;

But in her long, and hidden Course
Passing through the Earths darke veines,
Growes still from better unto worse,
And both her taste, and colour staines,

Then drilling on, learnes to encrease
False *Ecchoes*, and Confused sounds,
And unawares doth often seize
On veines of *Sulphur* under ground;

So poison'd, breaks forth in some Clime,
And at first sight doth many please,
But drunk, is puddle, or meere slime
And 'stead of Phisick, a disease;

Just such a tainted sink we have
Like that *Samaritans* dead *well*,
Nor must we for the Kernell crave
Because most voices like the *shell*.

Heale then these waters, Lord; or bring thy flock,
Since these are troubled, to the springing rock,
Looke downe great Master of the feast; O shine,
And turn once more our *water* into *wine*!

Cant. cap.4. ver.12.

My sister, my spouse is as a garden Inclosed, as a Spring shut up, and a fountain sealed up.

The

The Search.

'TIs now cleare day : I see a Rose
   Bud in the bright East, and disclose
The Pilgrim-Sunne ; all night have I
Spent in a roving Extasie
To find my Saviour ; I have been
As far as *Bethlem*, and have seen
His Inne, and Cradle ; Being there
I met the *Wise-men*, askt them where
He might be found, or what starre can
Now point him out, grown up a Man ?
To *Egypt* hence I fled, ran o're
All her parcht bosome to *Nile's* shore ,
Her yearly nurse ; came back, enquir'd
Amongst the *Doctors*, and desir'd
To see the *Temple*, but was shown
A little dust, and for the Town
A heap of ashes, where some sed
A small bright sparkle was a bed,
Which would one day (beneath the pole,)
Awake, and then refine the whole.

   Tyr'd here, I come to *Sychar* ; thence
To *Jacobs wel*, bequeathed since
Unto his sonnes, (where often they
In those calme, golden Evenings lay
Watring their flocks, and having spent
Those white dayes, drove home to the Tent
Their *well-fleec'd* traine;) And here(O fate !)
I sit, where once my Saviour sate ;
The angry Spring in bubbles swell'd
Which broke in sighes still, as they fill'd,
And whisper'd, *Jesus had been there*
But *Jacobs children would not heare.*
Loath hence to part, at last I rise
But with the fountain in my Eyes,
And here a fresh search is decreed
He must be found, where he did bleed ;

I walke the garden, and there see
Idea's of his Agonie,
And moving anguishments that set
His blest face in a bloudy sweat ;
I climb'd the Hill, perus'd the Crosse
Hung with my gaine, and his great losse,
Never did tree beare fruit like this,
Balsam of Soules, the bodyes blisse ;
But, O his grave ! where I saw lent
(For he had none,) a Monument,
An undefil'd, and new-heaw'd one,
But there was not the *Corner-stone* ;
Sure (then said I,) my Quest is vaine,
Hee'le not be found, where he was slaine,
So mild a Lamb can never be
'Midst so much bloud, and Crueltie ;
I'le to the Wildernesse, and can
Find beasts more mercifull then man,
He liv'd there safe, 'twas his retreat
From the fierce *Jew*, and *Herods* heat,
And forty dayes withstood the fell,
And high temptations of hell :
With Seraphins there talked he
His fathers flaming ministrie,
He heav'nd their *walks*, and with his eyes
Made those wild shades a Paradise,
Thus was the desert sanctified
To be the refuge of his bride ;
I'le thither then ; see, It is day,
The Sun's broke through to guide my way.
   But as I urg'd thus, and writ down
What pleasures should my Journey crown,
What silent paths, what shades, and Cells,
Faire, virgin-flowers, and hallow'd *Wells*
I should rove in, and rest my head
Where my deare Lord did often tread,
Sugring all dangers with successe,
Me thought I heard one singing thus ;

Leave

1.

Leave, leave thy gadding thoughts;
Who Pores
and spies
Still out of Doores
descries
Within them nought.

2.

The skinne, and shell of things
Though faire,
are not
Thy wish, nor Pray'r,
but got
By meere Despaire
of wings.

3.

To rack old Elements,
Or Dust;
and say
Sure here he must
needs stay
Is not the way,
nor Just.

Search well another world; who studies this,
Travels in Clouds, seekes *Manna*, where none is.

Acts Cap.17. ve.27,28.
*That they should seeke the Lord, if happily they might.
feele after him, and find him, though he be not far off from
every one of us, for in him we live, and move, and have our
being.*

B 2   *Isaac's*

Isaacs Marriage.

Gen.cap.24.ver.63.

And Isaac went out to pray in the field at the Even-tide,
and he lift up his eyes, and saw, and behold, the Camels
were comming.

PRaying ! and to be married ? It was rare,
  But now 'tis monstrous ; and that pious care
Though of our selves, is so much out of date,
That to renew't, were to degenerate.
But thou a Chosen sacrifice wert given,
And offer'd up so early unto heaven
Thy flames could not be out ; Religion was
Ray'd into thee, like beames into a glasse,
Where, as thou grewst, it multiply'd, and shin'd
The sacred Constellation of thy mind.
  But being for a bride, sure, prayer was
Very strange stuffe wherewith to court thy lasse,
Had'st ne'r an oath, nor Complement ? thou wert
An odde, corse sutor ; Hadst thou but the art
Of these our dayes, thou couldst have coyn'd thee twenty
New sev'rall oathes, and Complements (too) plenty ;
O sad, and wild excesse ! and happy those
White dayes, that durst no impious mirth expose !
When sinne, by sinning oft, had not lost sence,
Nor bold-fac'd custome banish'd Innocence ;
Thou hadst no pompous traine, nor *Antick* crowd
Of young, gay swearers, with their needless, lowd
Retinue ; All was here smooth as thy bride
And calme like her, or that mild Evening-tide ;
Yet, hadst thou nobler guests : Angels did wind,
And rove about thee, guardians of thy mind,
These fetch'd thee home thy bride, and all the way
Advis'd thy servant what to doe, and say ;
These taught him at the *well*, and thither brought
The Chast, and lovely object of thy thought ;

But

But here was ne'r a Complement, not one
Spruce, supple cringe, or study'd looke put on,
All was plaine, modest truth : Nor did she come
In *rowles*, and *Curles*, mincing, and stately dumbe,
But in a frighted, virgin-blush approach'd
Fresh as the morning, when 'tis newly Coach'd ;
O sweet, divine simplicity ! O grace
Beyond a Curled lock, or painted face !
A *Pitcher* too she had, nor thought it much
To carry that, which some would scorn to touch ;
With which in mild, chast language she did wooe
To draw him drinke, and for his Camels too.

   And now thou knewst her comming, It was time
To get thee wings on, and devoutly climbe
Unto thy God, for Marriage of all states
Makes most unhappy, or most fortunates ;
This brought thee forth, where now thou didst undresse
Thy soule, and with new pinions refresh
Her wearied wings, which so restor'd did flye
Above the stars, a track unknown, and high,
And in her piercing flight perfum'd the ayre
Scatt'ring the *Myrrbe*, and Incense of thy pray'r.
So from * *Lahai-roi's* Well, some spicie cloud
Woo'd by the Sun swels up to be his shrowd,
And from his moist wombe weeps a fragrant showre,
Which, scatter'd in a thousand pearls, each flowre
And herb partakes, where having stood awhile
And something coold the parch'd, and thirstie Isle,
The thankfull Earth unlocks her selfe, and blends,
A thousand odours, which (all mixt) she sends.
Up in one cloud, and so returnes the skies
That dew they lent, a breathing sacrifice.

   Thus soar'd thy soul, who (though young,) didst in-
Together with his bloud, thy fathers spirit,
Whose active zeale, and tryed faith were to thee
Familiar ever since thy Infancie,
Others were tym'd, and train'd up to't, but thou
Didst thy swift years in piety out-grow,

* *A wel
the Sou
Country
where Ja-
cob dwel
betweene
Cadesh,
& Bered
Heb. the
(herit wel of bi-
that livet
and seeth
me.*

B 3

Age

Age made them rev'rend, and a snowie head,
But thou wert so, e're time his snow could shed ;
Then, who would truly limne thee out, must paint
First, a *young Patriarch*, then a *marry'd Saint.*

The
Brittish Church.

A H ! he is fled !
And while these here their *mists*, and *shadowes* hatch,
My glorious head
Doth on those hills of Myrrhe, and Incense watch.
Hast, hast my deare,
The Souldiers here
Cast in their lotts againe,
That seamless coat
The Iewes touch'd not,
These dare divide, and staine.

2.

O get thee wings !
Or if as yet (untill these clouds depart,
And the day springs,)
Thou think'st it good to tarry where thou art,
Write in thy bookes
My ravish'd looks
Slain flock, and pillag'd fleeces,
And haste thee so
As a young Roe
Upon the mounts· of spices.

O Rosa Campi ! O lilium Convallium ! quomodò nunc
facta es pabulum Aprorum !

The

The Lampe.

'TIs dead night round about : Horrour doth creepe
   And move on with the shades ; stars nod, and sleepe,
And through the dark aire spin a firie thread
Such as doth gild the lazie glow-worms bed.
   Yet, burn'st thou here, a full day ; while I spend
My rest in Cares, and to the dark world lend
These flames, as thou dost thine to me ; I watch
That houre, which must thy life, and mine dispatch ;
But still thou doest out-goe me, I can see
Met in thy flames, all acts of piety ;
Thy light, is *Charity* ; Thy heat, is *Zeale* ;
And thy aspiring, active fires reveale
Devotion still on wing ; Then, thou dost weepe
Still as thou burn'st, and the warme droppings creepe
To measure out thy length, as if thou'dst know
What stock, and how much time were left thee now ;
Nor dost thou spend one teare in vain, for still
As thou dissolv'st to them, and they distill,
They're stor'd up in the socket, where they lye,
When all is spent, thy last, and sure supply,
And such is true repentance, ev'ry breath
Wee spend in sighes, is treasure after death ;
Only, one point escapes thee ; That thy Oile
Is still out with thy flame, and so both faile ;
But whensoe're I'm out, both shalbe in,
And where thou mad'st an end, there I'le begin.

Mark' Cap.13.ver.35.
Watch you therefore, for you know not when the master
of the house commeth, at Even, or at mid-night, or at the
Cock-crowing, or in the morning.

Mans

Mans fall, and Recovery.

FArewell you Everlasting hills! I'm Cast
   Here under Clouds, where stormes, and tempests blast
      This sully'd flowre
Rob'd of your Calme, nor can I ever make
Transplanted thus, one leafe of his t'awake,
      But ev'ry houre
He sleepes, and droops, and in this drowsie state
Leaves me a slave to passions, and my fate;
      Besides I've lost
A traine of lights, which in these Sun-shine dayes
Were my sure guides, and only with me stayes
      (Unto my cost,)
One sullen beame, whose charge is to dispense
More punishment, than knowledge to my sense;
      Two thousand yeares
I sojourn'd thus; at last *Jeshuruns* king
Those famous tables did from *Sinai* bring;
      These swell'd my feares,
Guilts, trespasses, and all this Inward Awe,
For sinne tooke strength, and vigour from the Law.
      Yet have I found
A plenteous way, (thanks to that holy one!)
To cancell all that e're was writ in stone,
      His saving wound
Wept bloud, that broke this Adamant, and gave
To sinners Confidence, life to the grave;
      This makes me span
My fathers journeys, and in one faire step
O're all their pilgrimage, and labours leap,
      For God (made man,)
Reduc'd th'Extent of works of faith; so made
Of their *Red Sea*, a *Spring*; I wash, they wade.

      Rom. Cap. 18. ver. 19.
As by the offence of one, the fault came on all men to con-
demnation; So by the Righteousness of one, the benefit aboun-
ded towards all men to the Justification of life.

                 The

The Showre.

'TWas so, I saw thy birth: That drowsie Lake
From her faint bosome breath'd thee, the disease
Of her sick waters, and Infectious Ease.
But, now at Even
Too grosse for heaven,
Thou fall'st in teares, and weep'st for thy mistake.

2.

Ah ! it is so with me; oft have I prest
Heaven with a lazie breath, but fruitles this
Peirc'd not; Love only can with quick accesse
Unlock the way,
When all else stray
The smoke, and Exhalations of the brest.

3.

Yet, if as thou doest melt, and with thy traine
Of drops make soft the Earth, my eyes could weep
O're my hard heart, that's bound up, and asleep;
Perhaps at last
(Some such showres past,)
My God would give a Sun-shine after raine.

Distraction

Diftraction.

O Knit me, that am crumbled duft ! the heape
    Is all difpers'd, and cheape ;
  Give for a handfull, but a thought
   And it is bought ;
    Hadft thou
Made me a ftarre, a pearle, or a rain-bow,
   The beames I then had fhot
   My light had leffend not,
    But now
I find my felfe the leffe, the more I grow ;
    The world
Is full of voices; Man is call'd, and hurl'd
   By each, he anfwers all,
   Knows ev'ry note, and call,
    Hence, ftill
Frefh dotage tempts, or old ufurps his will.
Yet, hadft thou clipt my wings, when Coffin'd in
  This quicken'd maffe of finne,
  And faved that light, which freely thou
    Didft then beftow,
    I feare
I fhould have fpurn'd, and faid thou didft forbeare ;
   Or that thy ftore was leffe,
   But now fince thou didft bleffe
    So much,
I grieve, my God ! that thou haft made me fuch.
    I grieve ?
O, yes ! thou know'ft I doe ; Come, and releive
  And tame, and keepe downe with thy light
  Duft that would rife, and dimme my fight,
   Left left alone too long
   Amidft the noife, and throng,
    Oppreffed I
Striving to fave the whole, by parcells dye.

       The

The Pursuite.

LOrd ! what a busie, restles thing
    Hast thou made man ?
Each day, and houre he is on wing,
    Rests not a span ;
Then, having lost the Sunne, and light
    By clouds surpriz'd
He keepes a Commerce in the night
    With aire disguis'd ;
Hadst thou given to this active dust
    A state untir'd,
The lost Sonne had not left the huske
    Nor home desir'd ;
That was thy secret, and it is
    Thy mercy too,
For when all failes to bring to blisse,
    Then, this must doe.
Ah ! Lord ! and what a Purchase will that be
To take us sick, that sound would not take thee ?

Mount of Olives.

SWeete, sacred hill ! on whose fair brow
  My Saviour sate, shall I allow
    Language to love
And Idolize some shade, or grove,
Neglecting thee ? such ill-plac'd wit,
Conceit, or call it what you please
    Is the braines fit,
    And meere disease ;

                2. *Cottswold,*

2.

Cotſwold, and *Coopers* both have met
With learned ſwaines, and Eccho yet
  Their pipes, and wit ;
But thou ſleep'ſt in a deepe neglect
Untouch'd by any ; And what need
The ſheep bleat thee a ſilly Lay
   That heard'ſt both reed
   And ſheepward play ?

3.

Yet, if Poets mind thee well
They ſhall find thou art their hill,
  And fountaine too,
Their Lord with thee had moſt to doe ;
He wept once, walkt whole nights on thee,
And from thence (his ſuff'rings ended,)
   Unto glorie
   Was attended ;

4.

Being there, this ſpacious ball
Is but his narrow footſtoole all,
  And what we thinke
Unſearchable, now with one winke
He doth compiſe ; But in this aire
When he did ſtay to beare our Ill
   And ſinne, this Hill
   Was then his Chaire.

The

The Incarnation, and Passion.

LOrd! when thou didst thy selfe undresse
  Laying by thy robes of glory,
To make us more, thou wouldst be lesse,
And becam'st a wofull story.

To put on Clouds instead of light,
And cloath the morning-starre with dust,
Was a translation of such height
As, but in thee, was ne'r exprest;

Brave wormes, and Earth! that thus could have
A God Enclos'd within your Cell,
Your maker pent up in a grave,
Life lockt in death, heav'n in a shell;

Ah, my deare Lord! what couldst thou spye
In this impure, rebellious clay,
That made thee thus resolve to dye
For those that kill thee every day?

O what strange wonders could thee move
To slight thy precious bloud, and breath!
Sure it was *Love*, my Lord; for *Love*
Is only stronger far than death.

The

The Call.

COme my heart ! come my head
In sighes, and teares !
'Tis now, since you have laine thus dead
Some twenty years ;
Awake, awake,
Some pitty take
Upon your selves ———
Who never wake to grone, nor weepe,
Shall be sentenc'd for their sleepe.

· 2.

Doe but see your sad estate,
how many sands
Have left us, while we careles sate
With folded hands ;
What stock of nights,
Ot dayes, and yeares
In silent flights
Stole by our eares,
How ill have we our selves bestow'd
Whose suns are all set in a Cloud ?

3.

Yet, come, and let's peruse them all ;
And as we passe,
What sins on every minute fall
Score on the glasse ;
Then weigh, and rate
Their heavy State
Untill
The glasse with teares you fill ;
That done, we shalbe safe, and good,
Those beasts were cleane, that chew'd the Cud.

Thou

¶

THou that know'st for whom I mourne,
    And why these teares appeare,
That keep'st account, till he returne
    Of all his dust left here;
As easily thou mightst prevent
    As now produce these teares,
And adde unto that day he went
    A faire supply of yeares.
But 'twas my sinne that forc'd thy hand
    To cull this *Prim-rose* out,
That by thy early choice forewarn'd
    My soule might looke about.
O what a vanity is man !
    How like the Eyes quick winke
His Cottage failes; whose narrow span
    Begins even at the brink !
Nine months thy hands are fashioning us,
    And many yeares (alas!)
E're we can lisp, or ought discusse
    Concerning thee, must passe ;
Yet have I knowne thy slightest things
    A *feather*, or a *shell*,
A *stick*, or *Rod* which some Chance brings
    The best of us excell,
Yea, I have knowne these shreds out last
    A faire-compacted frame
And for one *Twenty* we have past
    Almost outlive our name.
Thus hast thou plac'd in mans outside
    Death to the Common Eye,
That heaven within him might abide,
    And close eternitie ;

Hence,

Hence, youth, and folly (mans first shame,)
    Are put unto the slaughter,
And serious thoughts begin to tame
    The wise-mans-madnes *Laughter*;
Dull, wretched wormes! that would not keepe
    Within our first faire bed,
But out of *Paradise* must creepe
    For ev'ry foote to tread;
Yet, had our Pilgrimage bin free,
    And smooth without a thorne,
Pleasures had foil'd Eternitie,
    And *tares* had choakt the *Corne.*
Thus by the Crosse Salvation runnes,
    Affliction is a mother,
Whose painfull throws yield many sons,
    Each fairer than the other;
A silent teare can peirce thy throne,
    When lowd Joyes want a wing,
And sweeter aires streame from a grone,
    Than any arted string;
Thus, Lord, I see my gaine is great,
    My losse but little to it,
Yet something more I must intreate
    And only thou canst doe it.
O let me (like him,) know my End!
    And be as glad to find it,
And whatsoe'r thou shalt Commend,
    Still let thy Servant mind it!
Then make my soule white as his owne,
    My faith as pure, and steddy,
And deck me, Lord, with the same Crowne
    Thou hast crownd him already!

Vanity

Vanity of Spirit.

QUite spent with thoughts I left my Cell, and lay
  Where a shrill spring tun'd to the early day.
    I beg'd here long, and gron'd to know
    Who gave the Clouds so brave a bow,
    Who bent the spheres, and circled in
    Corruption with this glorious Ring,
    What is his name, and how I might
    Descry some part of his great light.
I summon'd nature : peirc'd through all her store,
Broke up some seales, which none had touch'd before,
    Her wombe, her bosome, and her head
    Where all her secrets lay a bed
    I rifled quite, and having past
    Through all the Creatures, came at last
    To search my selfe, where I did find
    Traces, and sounds of a strange kind.
Here of this mighty spring, I found some drills,
With Ecchoes beaten from th' eternall hills ;
    Weake beames, and fires flash'd to my sight,
    Like a young East, or Moone-shine night,
    Wich shew'd me in a nook cast by
    A peece of much antiquity,
    With Hyerogliphicks quite dismembred,
    And broken letters scarce remembred.
I tooke them up, and (much joy'd,) went about
T' unite those peeces, hoping to find out
    The mystery ; but this neer done,
    That little light I had was gone :
    It griev'd me much. At last, said I,
    Since in these veyls my Ecclips'd Eye
    May not approach thee, (for at night
    Who can have commerce with the light ?)
    I'le disapparell, and to buy
    But one half glaunce, most gladly dye.
       C

The

The Retreate.

HApy those early dayes! when I
    Shin'd in my Angell-infancy.
Before I understood this place
Appointed for my second race,
Or taught my soul to fancy ought
But a white, Celestiall thought,
When yet I had not walkt above
A mile, or two, from my first love,
And looking back (at that short space,)
Could see a glimpse of his bright-face ;
When on some *gilded Cloud*, or *flowre*
My gazing soul would dwell an houre,
And in those weaker glories spy
Some shadows of eternity ;
Before I taught my tongue to wound
My Conscience with a sinfull sound,
Or had the black art to dispence
A sev'rall sinne to ev'ry sence,
But felt through all this fleshly dresse
Bright *shootes* of everlastingnesse.
    O how I long to travell back
And tread again that ancient track !
That I might once more reach that plaine,
Where first I left my glorious traine,
From whence th' Inlightned spirit sees
That shady City of Palme trees ;
But (ah!) my soul with too much stay
Is drunk, and staggers in the way.
Some men a forward motion love,
But I by backward steps would move,
And when this dust falls to the urn
In that state I came return.

❡ Come

¶

Come, come, what doe I here?
  Since he is gone
Each day is grown a dozen year,
    And each houre, one;
    Come, come!
    Cut off the sum,
    By these soil'd teares!
    (Which only thou
    Know'st to be true,)
    Dayes are my feares.

2.

Ther's not a wind can stir,
    Or beam passe by,
But strait I think (though far,)
    Thy hand is nigh;
    Come, come!
    Strike these lips dumb:
    This restles breath
    That soiles thy name,
    Will ne'r be tame
    Untill in death.

3.

Perhaps some think a tombe
    No house of store,
But a dark, and seal'd up wombe,
    Which ne'r breeds more.
    Come, come!
    Such thoughts benum;
    But I would be
    With him I weep
    A bed, and sleep
    To wake in thee.

C 2

Mid-night

¶

Midnight.

WHen to my Eyes
(Whilst deep sleep others catches,)
Thine hoast of spyes
The starres shine in their watches,
I doe survey
Each busie Ray,
And how they work, and wind,
And wish each beame
My soul doth streame,
With the like ardour shin'd;
What Emanations,
Quick vibrations
And bright stirs are there ?
What thin Ejections,
Cold Affections,
And slow motions here ?

2.

Thy heav'ns (some say,)
Are a firie-liquid light,
Which mingling aye
Streames, and flames thus to the sight.
Come then, my god !
Shine on this bloud,
And water in one beame,
And thou shalt see
Kindled by thee
Both liquors burne, and streame.

○

O what bright quicknes,
  Active brightnes,
And celestiall flowes
  Will follow after
  On that water,
Which thy spirit blowes!

Math. Cap. 3. ver. xi.

I indeed baptize you with water unto repentance, but he that commeth after me, is mightier than I, whose shooes I am not worthy to beare, he shall baptize you with the holy Ghost, and with fire.

¶ Content.

PEace, peace! I know 'twas brave,
  But this corse fleece
I shelter in, is slave
  To no such peece.
  When I am gone,
I shall no ward-robes leave
  To friend, or sonne
But what their own homes weave,

2.

Such, though not proud, nor full,
  May make them weep,
And mourn to see the wooll
  Outlast the sheep ;
  Poore, Pious weare !
Hadst thou bin rich, or fine
  Perhaps that teare
Had mourn'd thy losse, not mine.

C 3   3. Why

3.

Why then these curl'd, puff'd points,
  Or a laced story ?
Death sets all out of Joint
  And scornes their glory ;
   Some Love a *Rose*
In hand, some in the skin ;
   But crosse to those,
I would have mine *within.*

¶

JOy of my life ! while left me here,
  And still my Love !
How in thy absence thou dost steere
  Me from above !
   A life well lead
   This truth commends,
   With quick, or dead
   It never ends.

2,

Stars are of mighty use : The night
  Is dark, and long ;
The Rode foul, and where one goes right,
  Six may go wrong.
   One twinkling ray
   Shot o'r some cloud,
   May clear much way
   And guide a croud.

3. Gods

3.

Gods Saints are ſhining lights : who ſtays
    Here long muſt paſſe.
O're dark hills, ſwiſt ſtreames, and ſteep ways
    As ſmooth as glaſſe ;
    But theſe all night
    Like Candles, ſhed
    Their beams, and light
    Us into Bed.

4.

They are (indeed,) our Pillar-fires
    Seen as we go,
They are that Cities ſhining ſpires
    We travell too ;
    A ſwordlike gleame
    Kept man for ſin
    Firſt *Out* ; This beame
    Will guide him *In.*

The Storm.

I See thouſe : and know my bloud
    Is not a Sea,
But a ſhallow, bounded floud
    Though red as he ;
Yet have I flows, as ſtrong as his,
    And boyling ſtremes that rave
With the ſame curling force, and hiſſe,
    As doth the mountain'd wavt,

But

2.

But when his waters billow thus,
   Dark storms, and wind
Incite them to that fierce discusse,
   Else not Inclin'd,
Thus the Enlarg'd, inraged air
   Uncalmes these to a floud,
But still the weather that's most fair
   Breeds tempests in my bloud ;

3.

Lord, then round me with weeping **Clouds**,
   And let my mind
In quick blasts sigh beneath those shrouds
   A spirit-wind,
So shall that storme purge this *Recluse*
   Which sinfull ease made foul ,
And *wind*, and *water* to thy use
   Both *wash*, and *wing* my soul.

The Morning-watch.

O Joyes ! Infinite sweetnes ! with what flowres,
 And shoots of glory, my soul breakes, and buds !
   All the long houres
   Of night, and Rest
   Through the still shrouds
   Of sleep, and Clouds,
  This Dew fell on my Breast ;
   O how it *Blouds*,

          And

And *Spirits* all my Earth ! heark ! In what *Rings,*
And *Hymning Circulations* the quick world
                    Awakes, and sings ;
                    The rising winds,
                    And falling springs,
                    Birds, beasts, all things
                Adore him in their kinds.
                    Thus all is hurl'd
In sacred *Hymnes,* and *Order,* The great *Chime*
And *Symphony* of nature. Prayer is
                    The world in tune,
                    A spirit-voyce,
                    And vocall joyes
                Whose *Eccho is* heav'ns blisse.
                    O let me climbe
When I lye down ! The Pious soul by night
Is like a clouded starre, whose beames though sed
                    To shed their light
                    Under some Cloud
                    Yet are above,
                    And shine, and move
                Beyond that mistic shrowd.
                    So in my Bed
That Curtain'd grave, though sleep, like ashes, hide
My lamp, and life, both shall in thee abide.

The Evening-watch.

A Dialogue.

Farewell ! I goe to sleep ; but when   *Body.*
    The day-star springs, I'le wake agen.

    Goe, sleep in peace ; and when thou lyest   *Soul.*
Unnumber'd in thy dust, when all this frame
Is but one dramme, and what thou now descriest
    In sev'rall parts shall want a name,

                                                        Then

Then may his peace be with thee, and each dust
Writ in his book, who ne'r betray'd mans trust !

    Amen ! but hark, e'r we two stray,   *Body.*
    How many hours do'st think 'till day ?

    Ah ! go ; th'art weak, and sleepie. Heav'n   *Soul.*
Is a plain watch, and without figures winds
All ages up ; who drew this Circle even
    He fils it ; Dayes, and hours are *Blinds.*
Yet, this take with thee ; The last gasp of time
Is thy first breath, and mans *eternall Prime.*

¶

SIlence, and stealth of dayes ! 'tis now
    Since thou art gone,
Twelve hundred houres, and not a brow
    But Clouds hang on.
As he that in some Caves thick damp
    Lockt from the light,
Fixeth a solitary lamp,
    To brave the night,
And walking from his Sun, when past
    That glim'ring Ray
Cuts through the heavy mists in haste
    Back to his day,
So o'r fled minutes I retreat
    Unto that hour
Which shew'd thee last, but did defeat
    Thy light, and pow'r,
I search, and rack my soul to see
    Those beams again,
But nothing but the snuff to me
    Appeareth plain ;
That dark, and dead sleeps in its known,
    And common urn,
But those fled to their Makers throne,
    There shine, and burn ;

D

O could I track them ! but souls muſt
Track one the other,
And now the ſpirit, not the duſt
Muſt be thy brother.
Yet I have one *Pearle* by whoſe light
All things I ſee,
And in the heart of Earth, and night
Find Heaven, and thee.

Church-Service.

BLeſt be the God of Harmony, and Love !
The God above !
And holy dove !
Whoſe Interceding, ſpirituall grones
Make reſtleſs mones
For duſt, and ſtones,
For duſt in every part,
But a hard, ſtonic heart.

2

O how in this thy Quire of Souls I ſtand
(Propt by thy hand)
A heap of ſand !
Which buſie thoughts (like winds) would ſcatter quite
And put to flight,
But for thy might ;
Thy hand alone doth tame
Thoſe blaſts, and knit my frame,

3.

So that both ſtones, and duſt, and all of me
Joyntly agree
To cry to thee,
And in this Muſick by thy Martyrs bloud
Seal'd, and made good
Preſent, O God !
The Eccho of theſe ſtones
—— My ſighes, and grones.

Buriall.

Buriall.

O Thou! the first fruits of the dead,
          And their dark bed,
When I am cast into that deep
          And senseless sleep
          The wages of my sinne,
              O then,
Thou great Preserver of all men!
          Watch o're that loose
          And empty house,
          Which I sometimes liv'd in.

2.

It is (in truth!) a ruin'd peece
          Not worth thy Eyes,
And scarce a room but wind, and rain
          Beat through, and stain
          The seats, and Cells within;
              Yet thou
Led by thy Love wouldst stoop thus low,
          And in this Cott
          All filth, and spott,
          Didst with thy servant Inne.

3.

And nothing can, I hourely see,
          Drive thee from me,
Thou art the same, faithfull, and just
          In life, or Dust;
          Though then (thus crumm'd) I stray
              In blasts,
Or Exhalations, and wasts
          Beyond all Eyes
          Yet thy love spies
          That Change, and knows thy Clay.

                              The

4.

The world's thy boxe : how then (there tost,)
            Can I be lost ?
But the delay is all ; Tyme now
            Is old, and flow,
                His wings are dull, and fickly ;
                    Yet he
Thy fervant is, and waits on thee,
            Cutt then the fumme,
            Lord hafte, Lord come,
    O come Lord *Jefus* quickly !

Rom. Cap. 8. ver. 23.
And not only they, but our felves alfo, which have the firft
fruits of the fpirit, even wee our felves grone within our
felves, waiting for the adoption, to wit, the redemption of
our body.

Chearfulnefs.

LOrd, with what courage, and delight
        I doe each thing
When thy leaft breath fuftaines my wing !
            I fhine, and move
            Like thofe above,
                And (with much gladneffe
                Quitting fadneffe,)
Make me faire dayes of every night.

2.

Affliction thus, meere pleafure is,
            And hap what will,
If thou be in't, 'tis welcome ftill ;
            But fince thy rayes
            In Sunnie dayes
                Thou doft thus lend
                And freely fpend,
Ah ! what fhall I return for this ?

3.

O that I were all Soul ! that thou
  Wouldst make each part,
Of this poor, sinfull frame pure heart !
  Then would I drown
  My single one,
  And to thy praise
  A Consort raise
Of *Hallelujahs* here below.

¶

SUre, there's a tye of Bodyes ! and as they
  Dissolve (with it,) to Clay,
Love languisheth, and memory doth rust
  O'r-cast with that cold dust ;
For things thus *Center'd*, without *Beames*, or *Action*
  Nor give, nor take *Contaction*,
And man is such a Marygold, these fled,
  That shuts, and hangs the head.

2.

Absents within the Line Conspire, and *Sense*
  Things distant doth unite,
Herbs sleep unto the *East*, and some fowles thence
  Watch the Returns of light ;
But hearts are not so kind : false, short delights
  Tell us the world is brave,
And wrap us in Imaginary flights
  Wide of a faithfull grave ;
Thus *Lazarus* was carried out of town ;
  For 'tis our foes chief art
By distance all good objects first to drown,
  And then besiege the heart.
But I will be my own *Deaths-head* ; and though
  The flatt'rer say, *I live*,
Because Incertainties we cannot know
  Be sure, not to believe.

        Peace,

Peace.

MY Soul, there is a Countrie.
　　Far beyond the ftars,
Where ftands a winged Centrie
　　All skilfull in the wars,
There above noife, and danger
　　Sweet peace fits crown'd with finiles,
And one born in a Manger
　　Commands the Beauteous files,
He is thy gracious friend,
　　And (O my Soul awake!)
Did in pure love defcend
　　To die here for thy fake,
If thou canft get but thither,
　　There growes the flowre of peace,
The Rofe that cannot wither,
　　Thy fortreffe, and thy eafe;
Leave then thy foolifh ranges;
　　For none can thee fecure,
But one, who never changes,
　　Thy God, thy life, thy Cure.

The Paffion.

O My chief good!
　　My dear, dear God!
When thy bleft bloud
Did Iffue forth forc'd by the Rod,
　　What pain didft thou
　　Feel in each blow!
　　How didft thou weep,
　　And thy felf fteep

In thy own precious, saving teares !
What cruell smart
Did teare thy heart !
How didst thou grone it
In the spirit,
O thou, whom my soul Loves, and feares !

2.

Most blessed Vine !
Whose juice so good
I feel as Wine,
But thy faire branches felt as bloud,
How wert thou prest
To be my feast !
In what deep anguish
Didst thou languish,
What springs of Sweat, and bloud did drown thee !
How in one path
Did the full wrath
Of thy great Father
Crowd, and gather,
Doubling thy griefs, when none would own thee !

3.

How did the weight
Of all our sinnes,
And death unite
To wrench, and Rack thy blessed limbes !
How pale, and bloudie
Lookt thy Body !
How bruis'd, and broke
With every stroke !
How meek, and patient was thy spirit !
How didst thou cry,
And grone on high
Father forgive,
And let them live,
I dye to make my foes inherit !

4.

O blessed Lamb!
That took'st my sinne;
That took'st my shame
How shall thy dust thy praises sing!
I would I were
One hearty tear!
One constant spring!
Then would I bring
Thee two small mites, and be at strife
Which should most vie,
My heart, or eye,
Teaching my years
In smiles, and tears
To weep, to sing, thy *Death,* my *Life.*

Rom:Cap.8.ver.19.

Etenim res Creatæ exerto Capite observantes expectant reve-
lationem Filiorum Dei.

ANd do they so? have they a Sense
Of ought but Influence?
Can they their heads lift, and expect,
And grone too? why th'Elect
Can do no more: my volumes sed
They were all dull, and dead,
They judg'd them senslesse, and their state
Wholly Inanimate.
Go, go; Seal up thy looks,
And burn thy books.

2.

I would I were a stone, or tree,
Or flowre by pedigree,
Or some poor high-way herb, or Spring
To flow, or bird to sing!

D

Then should I (tyed to one sure state,)
     . All day expect my date;
But I am sadly loose, and stray
     A giddy blast each way ;
     O let me not thus range !
      Thou canst not change.

3.

Sometimes I sit with thee, and tarry
     An hour, or so, then vary.
Thy other Creatures in this Scene
     Thee only aym, and mean;
Some rise to seek thee, and with heads
     Erect peep from their beds ;
Others, whose birth is in the tomb,
     And cannot quit the womb,
     Sigh there, and grone for thee,
      Their liberty.

4.

O let not me do lesse ! shall they
     Watch, while I sleep, or play ?
Shall I thy mercies still abuse
     With fancies, friends, or newes?
O brook it not ! thy bloud is mine,
     And my soul should be thine ;
O brook it not ! why wilt thou stop
     After whole showres one drop ?
     Sure, thou wilt joy to see
      Thy sheep with thee.

The

The Relapse.

MY God, how gracious art thou ! I had slipt
Almost to hell,
And on the verge of that dark, dreadful pit
Did hear them yell,
But O thy love ! thy rich, almighty love
That sav'd my soul,
And checkt their furie, when I saw them move,
And heard them howl ;
O my sole Comfort, take no more these wayes,
This hideous path,
And I wil mend my own without delayes,
Cease thou thy wrath !
I have deserv'd a thick, Egyptian damp,
Dark as my deeds,
Should *mist* within me, and put out that lamp
Thy spirit feeds ;
A darting Conscience full of stabs, and fears ;
No shade but *Yewgh*,
Sullen, and sad Ecclipses, Cloudie spheres,
These are my due.
But he that with his bloud, (a price too deere,)
My scores did pay,
Bid me, by vertue from him, chalenge here
The brightest day ;
Sweet, downie thoughts; soft *Lilly*-shades; Calm streams;
Joyes full, and true ;
Fresh, spicie mornings ; and eternal beams
These are his due.

EDINBURGH UNIVERSITY LIBRARY
WITHDRAWN

The Resolve.

I Have consider'd it; and find
   A longer stay
Is but excus'd neglect. To mind
   One path, and stray
Into another, or to none,
   Cannot be love;
When shal that traveller come home,
   That will not move?
If thou wouldst thither, linger not,
   Catch at the place,
Tell youth, and beauty they must rot,
   They'r but a *Case*;
Loose, parcell'd hearts wil freeze; The Sun
   With scatter'd locks
Scarce warms, but by contraction
   Can heat rocks;
Call in thy *Powers*; run, and reach
   Home with the light,
Be there, before the shadows stretch,
   And *Span* up night;
Follow the *Cry* no more: there is
   An ancient way
All strewed with flowres, and happiness
   And fresh as *May*;
There turn, and turn no more; Let wits,
   Smile at fair eies,
Or lips; But who there weeping sits,
   Hath got the *Prize*.

The

The Match.

DEar friend ! whose holy, ever-living lines
       Have done much good
    To many, and have checkt my blood,
My fierce, wild blood that still heaves, and inclines,
       But is still tam'd
    By those bright fires which thee inflam'd ;
Here I joyn hands, and thrust my stubborn heart
       Into thy *Deed*,
    There from no *Duties* to be freed,
And if hereafter *youth*, or *folly* thwart
       And claim their share,
  Here I renounce the pois'nous ware,

i i

ACcept, dread Lord, the poor Oblation,
       It is but poore,
    Yet through thy Mercies may be more.
O thou ! that canst not wish my souls damnation,
       Afford me life,
    And save me from all inward strife !
Two *Lifes* I hold from thee, my gracious Lord,
       Both cost thee deer,
    For one, I am thy Tenant here ;
The other, the true life, in the next world
       And endless is,
    O let me still mind *that* in *this* l
To thee therefore my *Thoughts*, *words*, *Actions*
       I do resign,
    Thy will in all be done, not mine.
Settle my *house*, and shut out all distractions
       That may unknit
    My heart, and thee planted in it ;

            D 3   Lord

Lord *Jesu*! thou didst bow thy blessed head
                        Upon a tree,
            O do as much, now unto me !
O hear, and heal thy servant ! Lord, strike dead
                    All lusts in me,
            Who onely wish life to serve thee ?
Suffer no more this dust to overflow
                        And drown my eies,
            But seal, or pin them to thy skies.
And let this *grain* which here in tears I sow
                    Though *dead*, and *sick*,
    Through thy *Increase* grow *new*, and *quick*.

Rules *and* Leſſons.

WHen first thy Eies unveil, give thy Soul leave
    To do the like ; our Bodies but forerun
The spirits duty ; True hearts spread, and heave
Unto their God, as flow'rs do to the Sun.
        Give him thy first thoughts then ; so shalt thou keep
        Him company all day, and in him sleep.

Yet, never sleep the Sun up ; Prayer shou'd
Dawn with the day ; There are set, awful hours
'Twixt heaven, and us ; The *Manna* was not good
After Sun-rising, far-day sullies flowres.
        Rise to prevent the Sun ; sleep doth sins glut,
        And heav'ns gate opens, when this world's is shut.

Walk with thy fellow-creatures : note the *bush*
And *whispers* amongst them. There's not a *Spring*,
Or *Leafe* but hath his *Morning-hymn* ; Each *Bush*
And *Oak* doth know *I AM* ; canst thou not sing ?
        O leave thy Cares, and follies ! go this way
        And thou art sure to prosper all the day.

Serve

Serve God before the world ; let him not go
Until thou haſt a bleſſing, then reſigne
The whole unto him ; and remember who
Prevail'd by *wreſtling* ere the *Sun* did *ſhine.*

  Poure *Oyle* upon the *ſtones,* weep for thy ſin,
  Then journey on, and have an eie to heav'n.

Mornings are *Myſteries* ; the firſt worlds *Youth,*
Mans *Reſurrection,* and the futures *Bud*
Shrowd in their births: The Crown of life, light, truth
Is ſtil'd their *ſtarre,* the *ſtone,* and *hidden food.*

  Three *bleſſings* wait upon them, two of which
  Should move ; They make us *holy, happy,* rich.

When the world's up, and ev'ry ſwarm abroad,
Keep thou thy temper, mix not with each Clay ;
Diſpatch neceſſities, life hath a load
Which muſt be carri'd on, and ſafely may.

  Yet keep thoſe cares without thee, let the heart
  Be Gods alone, and chooſe the better part.

Through all thy *Actions, Counſels,* and *Diſcourſe,*
Let *Mildneſs,* and *Religion* guide thee out,
If truth be thine, what needs a brutiſh force ?
But what's not *good,* and *juſt* ne'r go about.

  Wrong not thy Conſcience for a rotten ſtick,
  That gain is dreadful, which makes ſpirits ſick.

To God, thy Countrie, and thy friend be true,
If *Prieſt,* and *People* change, keep thou thy ground.
Who ſels Religion, is a *Judas Jew,*
And, oathes once broke, the ſoul cannot be ſound.

  The perjurer's a devil let looſe : what can
  Tie up his hands, that dares mock God, and man?

Seek not the ſame ſteps with the *Crowd* ; ſtick thou
To thy ſure trot ; a Conſtant, humble mind
Is both his own Joy, and his Makers too ;
Let folly duſt it on, or lag behind.

A sweet *self-privacy* in a right soul
Out-runs the Earth, and lines the utmost.pole.

To all that seek thee, bear an open heart;
Make not thy breast a *Labyrinth*, or *Trap*;
If tryals come, this wil make good thy part,
For honesty is safe, come what can hap;
    It is the good mans *feast*; The prince of flowres
    Which thrives in *storms*, and smels best after *showres*.

Seal not thy Eyes up from the poor, but give
Proportion to their *Merits*, and thy *Purse*;
Thou mai'st in Rags a mighty Prince relieve
Who, when thy sins call for't, can fence a Curse.
    Thou shalt not lose one *mite*. Though waters stray,
    The Bread we cast returns in fraughts one day.

Spend not an hour so, as to weep another,
For tears are not thine own; If thou giv'st words
Dash not thy *friend*, nor *Heav'n*; O smother
A vip'rous thought; some *Syllables* are *Swords*.
    Unbitted tongues are in their penance double,
    They shame their *owners*, and the *hearers* trouble.

Injure not modest bloud, whose *spirits* rise
In judgement against *Lewdness*; that's base wit
That voyds but *filth*, and *stench*. Hast thou no prize
But *sickness*, or *Infection*? stifle it.
    Who makes his jests of sins, must be at least
    If not a very *devill*, worse than a *Beast*.

Yet, fly no friend, if he be such indeed,
But meet to quench his *Longings*, and thy *Thirst*;
Allow your Joyes *Religion*; That done, speed
And bring the same man back, thou wert all first.
    Who so returns not, cannot pray aright,
    But shuts his door, and leaves God out all night.

To

To highten thy *Devotions*, and keep low
All mutinous thoughts, what busines e'r thou haft
Obferve God in his works ; here *fountains* flow,
Birds fing, *Beafts* feed, *Fifh* leap, and th'*Earth* ftands faft;
    Above are reftles *motions*, running *Lights*,
    Vaft Circling *Azure*, giddy *Clouds*, days, nights.

When *Seafons* change, then lay before thine Eys
His wondrous *Method* ; mark the various *Scenes*
In heav'n ; *Hail, Thunder, Rain-bows, Snow*, and *Ice*,
Calmes, Tempefts, Light, and *darknes* by his means ;
    Thou canft not mifle his Praife; Each *tree, herb, flowre*
    Are fhadows of his *wifedome*, and his Pow'r.

To *meales* when thou doeft come, give him the praife
Whofe *Arm* fupply'd thee ; Take what may *fuffice*,
And then be thankful ; O admire his ways
Who fils the worlds unempty'd granaries !
    A thankles feeder is a *Theif*, his feaft
    A very *Robbery*, and himfelf no *gueft.*

High-noon thus paft, thy time decays ; provide
Thee other thoughts ; Away with friends, and mirth ;
The Sun now ftoops, and hafts his beams to hide
Under the dark, and melancholy Earth.
    All but preludes thy End. Thou art the man
    Whofe *Rife, hight*, and *Defcent* is but   fpan.

Yet, fet as he doth, and 'tis well. Have all
Thy Beams home with thee : trim thy *Lamp*, buy *Oyl*,
And then fet forth ; who is thus dreft, The *Fall*
Furthers his glory, and gives death the foyl.
    Man is a *Summers day*; whofe *youth*, and *fire*
    Cool to a glorious *Evening*, and Expire.

When night comes, lift thy deeds ; make plain the way
'Twixt Heaven, and thee ; block it not with delays,
But perfect all before thou fleep'ft ; Then fay
Ther's one Sun more ftrung on my Bead of days.

                            What's

What's good ſcore up for Joy; The bad wel ſcann'd
Waſh off with tears, and get thy *Maſters* hand.

Thy Accounts thus made, ſpend in the grave one houre
Before thy time; Be not a ſtranger there
Where thou may'ſt ſleep whole ages; Lifes poor flowr
Laſts not a night ſometimes. Bad ſpirits fear
　　This Coverſation; But the good man lyes
　　Intombed many days before he dyes.

Being laid, and dreſt for ſleep, Cloſe not thy Eys
Up with thy Curtains; Give thy ſoul the wing
In ſome good thoughts; So when the day ſhall riſe
And thou *unrak'ſt* thy *fire*, thoſe *ſparks* will bring
　　New *flames*; Beſides where theſe lodge vain *heats* mourn
　　And die; That *Buſh* where God is, ſhall not burn.

When thy *Nap's* over, ſtir thy fire, unrake
In that *dead age*; one beam i'th' dark outvies
Two in the day; Then from the *Damps*, and *Ake*
Of night ſhut up thy *leaves*, be Chaſt; God prys
　　Through thickeſt nights; Though then the Sun be far
　　Do thou the works of *Day*, and riſe a *Star*.

Briefly, *Doe as thou would'ſt be done unto*,
Love God, and Love thy Neighbour; watch, and Pray.
Theſe are the *words*, and *works* of life; This do,
And live; who doth not thus, hath loſt *Heav'ns way.*
　　O loſe it not! look up, wilt Change thoſe *Lights*
　　For *Chains* of *Darknes*, and *Eternal Nights*?

　　　　　　　　　　　　　　　　Corruption

Corruption.

SUre, It was so. Man in those early days
    Was not all stone, and Earth,
He shin'd a little, and by those weak Rays
    Had some glimpse of his birth.
He saw Heaven o'r his head, and knew from whence
    He came (condemned,) hither,
And, as first Love draws strongest, so from hence
    His mind sure progress'd thither.
Things here were strange unto him : Swet, and till
    All was a thorn, or weed,
Nor did those last, but (like himself,) dyed still
    As soon as they did *Seed*,
They seem'd to quarrel with him ; for that Act
    That fel him, foyl'd them all,
He drew the Curse upon the world, and Crackt
    The whole frame with his fall.
This made him long for *home*, as loath to stay
    With murmurers, and foes;
He sigh'd for *Eden*, and would often say
    Ah ! what bright days were those ?
Nor was Heav'n cold unto him ; for each day
    The vally, or the Mountain
Afforded visits, and still *Paradise* lay
    In some green shade, or fountain.
Angels lay *Leiger* here ; Each Bush, and Cel,
    Each Oke, and high-way knew them,
Walk but the fields, or sit down at some *wel*,
    And he was sure to view them.
Almighty *Love* ! where art thou now ? mad man
    Sits down, and freezeth on,
He raves, and swears to stir nor fire, nor fan,
    But bids the thread be spun.

I see, thy Curtains are Close-drawn ; Thy bow
    Looks dim too in the Cloud,
Sin triumphs still, and man is sunk below
    The Center, and his shrowd ;
All's in deep sleep, and night ; Thick darknes lyes
    And hatcheth o'r thy people ;
But hark ! what trumpets that ? what Angel cries
    Arise ! Thrust in thy sickle.

H. Scriptures.

WElcome dear book, souls Joy, and food ! The feast
    Of Spirits, Heav'n extracted lyes in thee ;
    Thou art lifes Charter, The Doves spotless neast
Where souls are hatch'd unto Eternitie.

In thee the hidden stone, the *Manna* lies,
    Thou art the great *Elixir*, rare, and Choice ;
    The Key that opens to all Mysteries,
The *word* in Characters, God in the *Voice.*

O that I had deep Cut in my hard heart
    Each line in thee! Then would I plead in groans
    Of my Lords penning, and by sweetest Art
Return upon himself the *Law*, and *Stones.*
    Read here, my faults are thine. This Book, and I
    Will tell thee so ; *Sweet Saviour thou didst dye !*

Unprofitablenes

Unprofitablenes.

How rich, O Lord! how fresh thy visits are!
’Twas but just now my bleak leaves hopeles hung
    Sullyed with dust and mud;
Each snarling blast shot through me, and did share
Their Youth, and beauty, Cold showres nipt, and wrung
    Their spiçiness, and bloud;
But since thou didst in one sweet glance survey
Their sad decays, I flourish, and once more
    Breath all perfumes, and spice;
I smell a dew like *Myrrh*, and all the day
Wear in my bosome a full Sun; such store
    Hath one beame from thy Eys.
But, ah, my God! what fruit hast thou of this?
What one poor leaf did ever I yet fall
    To wait upon thy wreath?
Thus thou all day a thankless weed doest dress,
And when th’ hast done, a stench, or fog is all
    The odour I bequeath.

CHRISTS
Nativity.

Awake, glad heart! get up, and Sing,
  It is the Birth-day of thy King,
    Awake! awake!
    The Sun doth shake
Light from his locks, and all the way
Breathing Perfumes, doth spice the day.

                           Awake

2.

Awak, awak! heark, how th' *wood* rings,
winds whisper, and the busie *springs*
          A Consort make ;
          A wake, awake !
Man is their high-priest, and should rise
To offer up the sacrifice.

3.

I would I were some *Bird*, or Star,
Flutt'ring in woods, or lifted far
          Above this *Inne*
          And Rode of sin !
Then either Star, or *Bird*, should be
Shining, or singing still to thee.

4.

I would I had in my best part
Fit Roomes for thee ! or that my heart
          Were so clean as
          Thy manger was !
But I am all filth, and obscene,
Yet, if thou wilt, thou canst make clean.

5.

Sweet *Jesu* ! will then ; Let no more
This Leper haunt, and soyl thy door,
          Cure him, Ease him
          O, release him !
And let once more by mystick birth
The Lord of life be borne in Earth.

How

II.

HOw kind is heav'n to man ! If here
  One sinner doth amend
Strait there is Joy, and ev'ry sphere
  In musick doth Contend ;
And shall we then no voices lift ?
  Are mercy, and salvation
Not worth our thanks ? Is life a gift
  Of no more acceptation ?
Shal he that did come down from thence,
  And here for us was slain,
Shal he be now cast off ? no sense
  Of all his woes remain ?
Can neither Love, nor suff'rings bind ?
  Are we all stone, and Earth ?
Neither his bloudy passions mind,
  Nor one day blesse his birth ?
Alas, my God ! Thy birth now here
Must not be numbred in the year.

The Check.

PEace, peace ! I blush to hear thee ; when thou art
  A dusty story
A speechlesse heap, and in the midst my heart
  In the same livery drest
  Lyes tame as all the rest ;
When six years thence digg'd up, some youthfull Eie
  Seeks there for Symmetry
But finding none, shal leave thee to the wind,
  Or the next foot to Crush,
  Scatt'ring thy kind
And humble dust, tell then dear flesh
  Where is thy glory ?

As

2.

As he that in the midst of day Expects
  The hideous night,
Sleeps not, but shaking off sloth, and neglects,
    Works with the Sun, and sets
    Paying the day its debts ;
That (for Repose, and darknes bound,) he might
    Rest from the fears i'th' night ;
So should we too. All things teach us to die
    And point us out the way
      While we passe by
    And mind it not ; play not away
      Thy glimpse of light.

3.

View thy fore-runners : Creatures giv'n to be
    Thy youths Companions,
Take their leave, and die ; Birds, beasts, each tree
    All that have growth, or breath
    Have one large language, *Death*.
O then play not ! but strive to him, who Can
    Make these sad shades pure Sun,
Turning their mists to beams, their damps to day,
      Whose pow'r doth so excell
        As to make Clay
      A spirit, and true glory dwell
        In dust, and stones.

4.

Heark, how he doth Invite thee ! with what voice
    Of Love, and sorrow
He begs, and Calls ; *O that in these thy days*
    Thou knew'st but thy own good !
    Shall not the Crys of bloud,
Of Gods own bloud awake thee ? He bids beware
    Of drunknes, surfeits, Care,
But thou sleep'st on : wher's now thy protestation,
      Thy Lines, thy Love ? Away,
        Redeem the day ,
      The day that gives no observation,
        Perhaps to morrow.   Disorder

Diſorder *and* frailty.

WHen firſt thou didſt even from the grave
  And womb of darknes becken out
My brutiſh ſoul, and to thy ſlave
Becam'ſt thy ſelf, both guide, and Scout ;
    Even from that hour
Thou gotſt my heart ; And though here toſt
  By winds, and bit with froſt
      I pine, and ſhrink
      Breaking the link
'Twixt thee, and me ; And oftimes creep
Into th' old ſilence, and dead ſleep,
      Quitting thy way,
      All the long day,
Yet, ſure, my God ! I love thee moſt.
      Alas, thy love !

2.

I threaten heaven, and from my Cell
Of Clay, and frailty break, and bud
Touch'd by thy fire, and breath ; Thy bloud
Too, is my Dew, and ſpringing wel.
    But while I grow
And ſtretch to thee, ayming at all
  Thy ſtars, and ſpangled hall,
      Each fly doth taſt
      Poyſon, and blaſt
My yielding leaves ; ſometimes a ſhowr
Beats them quite off, and in an hour
      Not one poor ſhoot
      But the bare root
Hid under ground ſurvives the fall,
      Alas, frail weed !

E   *Thus*

3.

Thus like some sleeping Exhalation
(Which wak'd by heat, and beams, makes up
Unto that Comforter, the Sun,
And soars, and shines ; But e'r we sup
        And walk two steps
Cool'd by the damps of night, descends,
        And, whence it sprung, there ends,)
            Doth my weak fire
            Pine, and retire,
And (after all my hight of flames,)
In sickly Expirations tames
            Leaving me dead
            On my first bed
Untill thy Sun again ascends.
        Poor, falling Star !

4.

O, is ! but give wings to my fire,
And hatch my soul, untill it fly
Up where thou art, amongst thy tire
Of Stars, above Infirmity ;
        Let not perverse,
And foolish thoughts adde to my Bil
        Of forward sins, and Kil
            That seed, which thou
            In me didst sow,
But dresse, and water with thy grace
Together with the seed, the place ;
            And for his sake
            Who died to stake
His life for mine, tune to thy will
        My heart, my verse.

Hosea Cap. 6. ver. 4.

O Ephraim what shall I do unto thee ? O Judah, how shall I intreat thee ? for thy goodness is as a morning Cloud, and as the early Dew it goeth away.

Idle

Idle Verse.

GO, go, queint folies, sugred sin,
  Shadow no more my door;
I will no longer Cobwebs spin,
  I'm too much on the score.

For since amidst my youth, and night,
  My great preserver smiles,
Wee'l make a Match, my only light,
  And Joyn against their wiles;

Blind, desp'rate *fits*, that study how
  To dresse, and trim our shame,
That gild rank poyson, and allow
  Vice in a fairer name;

The *Purles* of youthfull bloud, and bowles,
  Lust in the Robes of Love,
The idle talk of feav'rish souls
  Sick with a scarf, or glove;

Let it suffice my warmer days
  Simper'd, and shin'd on you,
Twist not my Cypresse with your Bays,
  Or Roses with my Yewgh;

Go, go, seek out some greener thing,
  It snows, and freezeth here;
Let Nightingales attend the spring,
  Winter is all my year.

E 2

Son-dayes.

BRight shadows of true Rest ! some shoots of bliſſe,
    Heaven once a week ;
The next worlds gladnes prepoſſeſt in this ;
    A day to ſeek ;

Eternity in time ; the ſteps by which
We Climb above all ages ; Lamps that light
Man through his heap of dark days ; and the rich,
And full redemption of the whole weeks flight.

2.

The Pulleys unto headlong man ; times bower ;
    The narrow way ;
Tranſplanted Paradiſe ; Gods walking houre ;
    The Cool o'th' day ;

The Creatures *Jubile* ; Gods parle with duſt ;
Heaven here ; Man on thoſe hills of Myrrh, and flowres ;
Angels deſcending ; the Returns of Truſt ;
A Gleam of glory, after ſix-days-ſhowres.

3.

The Churches love-feaſts ; Times Prerogative,
    And Intereſt
Deducted from the whole; The Combs, and hive,
    And home of reſt.

The milky way Chalkt out with Suns ; a Clue
That guides through erring hours ; and in full ſtory
A taſte of Heav'n on earth ; the pledge, and Cue
Of a full feaſt ; And the Out-Courts of glory.

        Repentance

Repentance.

LOrd, since thou didst in this vile Clay
       That sacred Ray
Thy spirit plant, quickning the whole
With that one grains Infused wealth,
My forward flest creept on, and subtly stole
Both growth, and power; Checking the health
And heat of thine : That little gate
And narrow way, by which to thee
The Passage is, He term'd a grate
And Entrance to Captivitie ;
Thy laws but nets, where some small birds
(And those but seldome too) were caught,
Thy Promises but empty words
Which none but Children heard, or taught.
This I believed : And though a friend
Came oft from far, and whisper'd, *No* ;
Yet that not sorting to my end
I wholy listen'd to my foe.
Wherefore, pierc'd through with grief, my sad
Seduced soul sighs up to thee,
To thee who with true light art Clad
And seest all things just as they be.
Look from thy throne upon this Rowl
Of heavy sins, my high transgressions,
Which I Contesse withall my soul,
My God, Accept of my Confession.
       It was last day
(Touch'd with the guilt of my own way)
I sate alone, and taking up
       The bitter Cup,
Through all thy fair, and various store
Sought out what might outvie my score.
   The blades of grasse, thy Creatures feeding,
    The trees, their leafs ; the flowres, their seeding ;

                                     The

The Dust, of which I am a part,
The Stones much softer than my heart,
The drops of rain, the sighs of wind,
The Stars to which I am stark blind,
The Dew thy herbs drink up by night,
The beams they warm them at i'th' light,
All that have signature or life,
I summon'd to decide this strife,
And lest I should lack for Arrears,
A spring ran by, I told her tears,
But when these came unto the scale,
My sins alone outweigh'd them all.

O my dear God! my life, my love!
Most blessed lamb! and mildest dove!
Forgive your penitent Offender,
And no more his sins remember,
Scatter these shades of death, and give
Light to my soul, that it may live;
Cut me not off for my transgressions,
Wilful rebellions, and suppressions,
But give them in those streams a part
Whose spring is in my Saviours heart.
Lord, I confesse the heynous score,
And pray, I may do so no more,
Though then all sinners I exceed
O think on this; *Thy Son did bleed*;
O call to mind his wounds, his woes,
His Agony, and bloudy throws;
Then look on all that thou hast made,
And mark how they do fail, and fade,
The heavens themselves, though fair and bright
Are dark, and unclean in thy sight,
How then, with thee, Can man be holy
Who doest thine Angels charge with folly?
O what am I, that I should breed
Figs on a thorne, flowres on a weed!
I am the gourd of sin, and sorrow
Growing o'r night, and gone to morrow,

In

In all this *Round* of life and death
Nothing's more vile than is my breath,
Profanenes on my tongue doth rest,
Defects, and darknes in my brest,
Pollutions all my body wed,
And even my soul to thee is dead,
Only in him, on whom I feast,
Both soul, and body are well drest,
   His pure perfection quits all score,
   And fills the Boxes of his poor ;
He is the Center of long life, and light,
I am but finite, He is Infinite.
O let thy *Justice* then in him Confine,
And through his merits, make thy mercy mine.

The BURIAL
Of an Infant.

BLest Infant Bud, whose Blossome-life
  Did only look about, and fal,
Wearyed out in a harmles strife
Of tears, and milk, the food of all ;

Sweetly didst thou expire : Thy soul
Flew home unstain'd by his new kin,
For ere thou knew'st how to be foul,
Death *wean'd* thee from the world, and sin.

Softly rest all thy Virgin-Crums !
Lapt in the sweets of thy young breath,
Expecting till thy Saviour Comes
To *dresse* them, and *unswadle* death.

E 4

Faith

Faith.

BRight, and blest beame ! whose strong projection
        Equall to all,
Reacheth as well things of dejection
        As th' high, and tall ;
How hath my God by raying thee
        Inlarg'd his spouse,
And of a private familie
        Made open house ?
All may be now Co-heirs; no noise
        Of *Bond*, or *Free*
Can Interdict us from those Joys
        That wait on thee ,
The Law, and Ceremonies made
        A glorious night,
Where Stars, and Clouds, both light, and shade
        Had equal right ;
But, as in nature, when the day
        Breaks , night adjourns,
Stars shut up shop, mists pack away,
        And the Moon mourns ;
So when the Sun of righteousness
        Did once appear,
That Scene was chang'd, and a new dresse
        Left for us here;
Veiles became useles, Altars fel,
        Fires smoking die ;
And all that sacred pomp, and shel
        Of things did flie ;
Then did he shine forth, whose sad fall,
        And bitter fights
Were figur'd in those mystical,
        And Cloudie Rites ;

                                And

'And as i'th' natural Sun, these three,
   Light, motion, heat,
So are now *Faith, Hope, Charity*
   Through him Compleat ;
Faith spans up blisse ; what sin, and death
   Put us quite from,
Lest we should run for't out of breath,
   Faith brings us home ; ı
So that I need no more, but say
   I do believe,
And my most loving Lord straitway
   doth answer, *Live.*

The Dawning.

AH ! what time wilt thou come ? when shall that crie
   The *Bridegroome's Comming* ! fil the sky ?
   Shall it in the Evening run
   When our words and works are done ?
   Or wil thy all-surprizing light
      Break at midnight ?
When either sleep, or some dark pleasure
Possesseth mad man without measure ;
   Or shal these early, fragrant hours
      Unlock thy bowres ?
And with their blush of light descry
Thy locks crown'd with eternitie;
   Indeed, it is the only time
   That with thy glory doth best chime,
All now are stirring, ev'ry field
      Ful hymns doth yield,
The whole Creation shakes off night,
And for thy shadow looks the light,
   Stars now vanish without number,
   Sleepie Planets set, and slumber,

The purfie Clouds disband, and fcatter,
All expect fome fudden matter,
Not one beam triumphs, but from far
      That morning-ftar ;

O at what time foever thou
(Unknown to us,) the heavens wilt bow,
And, with thy Angels in the *Van*,
Defcend to Judge poor carelefs man,
Grant, I may not like puddle lie
In a Corrupt fecuritie,
Where, if a traveller water crave,
He finds it dead, and in a grave ;
But as this reftlefs, vocall *Spring*
All day, and night doth run, and fing,
And though here born, yet is acquainted
Elfewhere, and flowing keeps untainted ;
So let me all my bufie age
In thy free fervices ingage,
And though (while here) of force I muft
Have Commerce fomtimes with poor duft,
And in my flefh, though vile, and low,
As this doth in her Channel, flow,
Yet let my Courfe, my aym, my Love,
And chief acquaintance be above ;
So when that day, and hour fhal come
In which thy felf wil be the Sun,
Thou'lt find me dreft and on my way,
Watching the Break of thy great day.

Admiffion.

Admission.

How shril are silent tears? when sin got head
    And all my Bowels turn'd
To brasse, and iron ; when my stock lay dead,
    And all my powers mourn'd;
    Then did these drops (for Marble sweats,
      And Rocks have tears,)
   As rain here at our windows beats,
    Chide in thine Ears ;

2.

No quiet couldst thou have : nor didst thou wink,
    And let thy Begger lie,
But e'r my eies could overflow their brink
    Didst to each drop reply ;
    Bowels of Love ! at what low rate,
      And slight a price
   Dost thou relieve us at thy gate,
    And stil our Cries ?

3.

Wee are thy Infants, and suck thee ; If thou
    But hide, or turn thy face,
Because where thou art, yet, we cannot go,
    We send tears to the place,
    These find thee out, and though our sins
      Drove thee away,
   Yet with thy love that absence wins
    Us double pay.

4.

O give me then a thankful heart ! a heart
    After thy own, not mine ;
So after thine, that all, and ev'ry part
    Of mine, may wait on thine ;

O hear! yet not my tears alone,
 Hear now a floud,
A floud that drowns both tears, and grones,
 My Saviours bloud.

Praise.

KIng of Comforts! King of life!
 Thou haſt cheer'd me,
And when fears, and doubts were rife,
 Thou haſt cleer'd me!

Not a nook in all my Breaſt
 But thou fill'ſt it,
Not a thought, that breaks my reſt,
 But thou kill'ſt it;

Wherefore with my utmoſt ſtrength
 I wil praiſe thee,
And as thou giv'ſt line, and length,
 I wil raiſe thee;

Day, and night, not once a day
 I will bleſſe thee,
And my ſoul in new array
 I will dreſſe thee;

Not one minute in the year
 But I'l mind thee,
As my ſeal, and bracelet here
 I wil bind thee;

In thy word, as if in heaven
 I wil reſt me,
And thy promiſe 'til made even
 There ſhall feaſt me.

Then

Then, thy sayings all my life
          They shal please me,
And thy bloudy wounds, and strife
          They wil ease me ;

With thy grones my daily breath
          I will measure,
And my life hid in thy death
          I will treasure.

          Though then thou art
          Past thought of heart
All perfect fulness,
          And canst no whit
          Accesse admit
From dust and dulness ;

          Yet to thy name
          (as not the same
With thy bright Essence,)
          Our foul, Clay hands
          At thy Commands
Bring praise, and Incense ;

          If then, dread Lord,
          When to thy board
Thy wretch comes begging,
          He hath a flowre
          Or (to his pow'r,)
Some such poor Off'ring ;

          When thou hast made
          Thy begger glad,
And fill'd his bosome,
          Let him (though poor,)
          Strow at thy door
That one poor Blossome.

                              Dressing ?

Dressing.

O Thou that lovest a pure, and whitend soul !
That feedst among the Lillies, 'till the day
Break, and the shadows flee ; touch with one **Coal**
My frozen heart ; and with thy secret key

Open my desolate rooms ; my gloomie Brest
With thy cleer fire refine, burning to dust
These dark Confusions, that within me nest,
And soyl thy Temple with a sinful rust.

Thou holy, harmless, undefil'd high-priest !
The perfect, ful oblation for all sin,
Whose glorious conquest nothing can resist,
But even in babes doest triumph still and win ;

Give to thy wretched one
Thy mysticall *Communion*,
That, absent, he may see,
Live, die, and rise with thee ;
Let him so follow here, that in the end
He may take thee, as thou doest him intend,

Give him thy private seal,
Earnest, and sign ; Thy gifts so deal
That these forerunners here
May make the future cleer ;
Wherever thou dost bid, let faith make good,
Bread for thy body, and Wine for thy blood.
Give him (with pitty) love,
Two flowres that grew with thee above;
Love that shal not admit
Anger for one short fit,
And pitty of such a divine extent
That may thy members, more than mine, resent.

Give

Give me, my God! thy grace,
　The beams, and brightnes of thy face,
　　That never like a beast
　　I take thy sacred feast,
Or the dread mysteries of thy blest bloud
Use, with like Custome, as my Kitchin food.
　　Some sit to thee, and eat
　　Thy body as their Common meat,
　　　O let not me do so!
　　　Poor dust should ly still low,
Then kneel my soul, and body; kneel, and bow;
If *Saints*, and *Angels* fal down, much more thou.

Easter-day.

THou, whose sad heart; and weeping head lyes low,
　Whose Cloudy brest cold damps invade,
Who never feel'st the Sun, nor smooth'st thy brow,
　But sitt'st oppressed in the shade,
　　　　Awake, awake,
And in his Resurrection partake,
　　Who on this day (that thou might'st rise as he,)
　　Rose up, and cancell'd two deaths due to thee.

Awake, awake; and, like the Sun, disperse
　All mists that would usurp this day;
Where are thy Palmes, thy branches, and thy verse?
　Hosanna! heark; why doest thou stay?
　　　　Arise, arise,
And with his healing bloud anoint thine Eys,
　　Thy inward Eys; his bloud will cure thy mind,
　　Whose spittle only could restore the blind.

Easter.

Easter Hymn.

DEath, and darkneſs get you packing,
Nothing now to man is lacking,
All your triumphs now are ended,
And what *Adam* marr'd, is mended;
Graves are beds now for the weary,
Death a nap, to wake more merry;
Youth now, full of pious duty,
Seeks in thee for perfect beauty,
The weak, and aged tir'd, with length
Of daies, from thee look for new ſtrength,
And Infants with thy pangs Conteſt
As pleaſant, as if with the breſt;
   Then, unto him, who thus hath thrown
Even to Contempt thy kingdome down
And by his blood did us advance
Unto his own Inheritance,
To him be glory, power, praiſe,
From this, unto the laſt of daies.

The Holy Communion.

WElcome ſweet, and ſacred feaſt; welcome life!
   Dead I was, and deep in trouble;
But grace, and bleſſings came with thee ſo rife,
   That they have quicken'd even drie ſtubble;
      Thus ſoules their bodies animate,
      And thus, at firſt, when things were rude,
         Dark, void, and Crude
They, by thy Word, their beauty had, and date;
      All were by thee,
      And ſtil muſt be,
                                        Nothing

Nothing that is, or lives,
But hath his Quicknings, and reprieves
As thy hand opes, or shuts ;
Healings, and Cuts,
Darkness, and day-light, life, and death
Are but meer leaves turn'd by thy breath.
Spirits without thee die,
And blackness sits
On the divinest wits,
As on the Sun Ecclipses lie.
But that great darkness at thy death
When the veyl broke with thy last breath;
Did make us see
The way to thee ;
And now by these sure, sacred ties,
After thy blood
(Our sov'rain good,)
Had clear'd our eies,
And given us sight ;
Thou dost unto thy self betroth
Our souls, and bodies both
In everlasting light.

Was't not enough that thou hadst payd the price
And given us eies
When we had none, but thou must also take
Us by the hand
And keep us still awake,
When we would sleep,
Or from thee creep,
Who without thee cannot stand ?

Was't not enough to lose thy breath
And blood by an accursed death,
But thou must also leave
To us that did bereave
Thee of them both, these seals the means
That should both cleanse

F

And keep us so,
Who wrought thy wo ?
O rose of *Sharon* ! O the Lilly
Of the valley!
How art thou now, thy flock to keep,
Become both *food*, and *Shepheard* to thy sheep !

Psalm 121.

UP to those bright, and gladsome hils
    Whence flowes my weal, and mirth,
I look, and sigh for him, who fils
    (Unseen,) both heaven, and earth.

He is alone my help, and hope,
    that I shall not be moved,
His watchful Eye is ever ope,
    And guardeth his beloved;

The glorious God is my sole stay,
    He is my Sun, and shade,
The cold by night, the heat by day,
    Neither shall me invade.

He keeps me from the spite of foes,
    Doth all their plots controul,
And is a shield (not reckoning those,)
    Unto my very soul.

Whether abroad, amidst the Crowd,
    Or els within my door,
He is my Pillar, and my Cloud,
    Now, and for evermore.

Affliction.

Affliction.

PEace, peace ; It is not so. Thou doeſt miſcall
 Thy Phyſick ; Pils that change
Thy ſick Acceſſions into ſetled health,
This is the great *Elixir* that turns gall
To wine, and ſweetneſs; Poverty to wealth,
 And brings man home, when he doth range.
  Did not he, who ordain'd the day,
   Ordain night too ?
  And in the greater world diſplay
  What in the leſſer he would do ?
All fleſh is Clay, thou know'ſt ; and but that **God**
  Doth uſe his rod,
And by a fruitfull Change of froſts, and ſhowres
 Cheriſh, and bind thy *pow'rs*,
Thou wouldſt to weeds, and thiſtles quite diſperſe,
 And be more wild than is thy verſe ;
Sickneſs is wholſome, and Croſſes are but curbs
 To check the mule, unruly man,
They are heavens husbandry, the famous fan
 Purging the floor which Chaff diſturbs.
Were all the year one conſtant Sun-ſhine, wee
  ſhould have no flowres,
All would be drought, and leanneſs ; not a tree
  would make us bowres ;
Beauty conſiſts in colours ; and that's beſt
 Which is not fixt, but flies, and flowes
The ſettled *Red* is dull, and *whites* that reſt
 Something of ſickneſs would diſcloſe.
  Viciſſitude plaies all the game,
   nothing that ſtirrs,
   Or hath a name,
  But waits upon this wheel,
Kingdomes too have their Phyſick, and for ſteel,
 Exchange their peace, and furrs.

        Thus

Thus doth God *Key* diforder'd man
   (which none elfe can,)
Tuning his breft to rife, or fall ;
And by a facred, needfull art
  Like ftrings, ftretch ev'ry part
Making the whole moft Muficall.

The Tempeft.

HOw is man parcell'd out ? how ev'ry hour
   Shews him himfelf, or fomthing he fhould fee ?
  This late, long heat may his Inftruction be,
And tempefts have more in them than a fhowr.

    when nature on her bofome faw
      Her Infant's die,
   And all her flowres wither'd to ftraw,
     Her brefts grown dry ;
   She made the Earth their nurfe,& tomb,
     Sigh to the sky,
  'Til to thofe fighes fetch'd from her womb
     Rain did reply,
  So in the midft of all her fears
     And faint requefts
  Her Earneft fighes procur'd her tears
     And fill'd her brefts.

O that man could do fo ! that he would hear
   The world read to him ! all the vaft expence
  In the Creation fhed, and flav'd to fence
Makes up but lectures for his eie, and ear.

Sure, mighty love forefeeing the difcent
   Of this poor Creature, by a gracious art
  Hid in thefe low things fnares to gain his heart,
And layd furprizes in each Element.

               All

All things here ſhew him heaven ; *waters* that fall
    Chide, and fly up ; *Miſts* of corrupteſt ſome
    Quit their firſt beds & mount;trees,herbs,ſſowres,all
Strive upwards ſtil, and point him the way home.

How do they caſt off groſſneſs ? only *Earth*,
    And *Man* (like *Iſſachar*) in lodes delight,
    Water's refin'd to *Motion*, Aire to *Light*,   * *Light,*
Fire to all * three, but man hath no ſuch mirth.   *Motion,*
                                      heat.

Plants in the *root* with Earth do moſt Comply,
    Their *Leaſs* with water, and humiditie,
    The *Flowres* to air draw neer, and ſubtiltie,
And *ſeeds* a kinred fire have with the sky.

All have their *keyes*, and ſet *aſcents* ; but man
    Though he knows theſe, and hath more of his own,
    Sleeps at the ladders foot ; alas ! what can
Theſe new diſcoveries do, except they drown ?

Thus groveling in the ſhade, and darkneſs, he
    Sinks to a dead oblivion ; and though all
    He ſees, (like *Pyramids*,) ſhoot from this ball
And leſs'ning ſtill grow up inviſibly,

Yet hugs he ſtil his durt ; The *ſtuffe* he wears
    And painted trimming takes down both his eies,
    Heaven hath leſs beauty than the duſt he ſpies,
And money better muſick than the *Spheres.*

Life's but a blaſt, he knows it ; what ? ſhal ſtraw,
    And bul-ruſh-fetters temper his ſhort hour ?
    Muſt he nor ſip,nor ſing ? grows ne'r a flowr
To crown his temples ? ſhal dreams be his law ?

O fooliſh man ! how haſt thou loſt thy ſight ?
    How is it that the Sun to thee alone
    Is grown thick darkneſs, and thy bread, a ſtone ?
Hath fleſh no ſoftneſs now ? mid-day no light ?

                Lord !

Lord ! thou didst put a soul here ; If I must
  Be broke again, for flints will give no fire
  Without a steel, O let thy power cleer
Thy gift once more, and grind this flint to dust !

Retirement.

WHo on yon throne of Azure sits,
    Keeping close house
  Above the morning-starre,
    Whose meaner showes,
And outward utensils these glories are
    That shine and share
  Part of his mansion ; He one day
    When I went quite astray
      Out of meer love
      By his mild Dove
Did shew me home, and put me in the way.

2.

Let it suffice at length thy fits
    And lusts (said he,)
  Have had their wish, and way ;
    Presse not to be
Still thy own foe, and mine ; for to this day
    I did delay,
  And would not see, but chose to wink,
    Nay, at the very brink
      And edge of all
      When thou wouldst fall
My *love-twist* held thee up, my *unseen link*.

3.

I know thee well ; for I have fram'd
    And hate thee not,
Thy spirit too is mine ;
    I know thy lot,
Extent, and end, for my hands drew the line
    Assigned thine ;
If then thou would'st unto my seat,
    'Tis not th'applause, and feat
      Of dust, and clay
      Leads to that way,
But from those follies a resolv'd Retreat.

4.

Now here below where yet untam'd
    Thou doest thus rove
I have a house as well
    As there above,
In it my *Name*, and *honour* both do dwell
    And shall untill
I make all new ; there nothing gay
    In perfumes, or Array,
      Dust lies with dust
      And hath but just
The same Respect, and room, with ev'ry clay.

5.

A faithful school where thou maist see
    In Heraldrie
Of stones, and speechless Earth
    Thy true descent ;
Where dead men preach, who can turn feasts, and mirth
    To funerals, and *Lent*.
There dust that out of doors might fill
    Thy eies, and blind thee still,
      Is fast asleep ;
      Up then, and keep
Within those doors, (my doors) dost hear ? *I will.*

                        Love

Love, and Discipline.

Since in a land not barren stil
(Because thou dost thy grace distil,)
My lott is faln, Blest be thy will !

And since these biting frosts but kil
Some tares in me which choke, or spil
That seed thou sow'st, Blest be thy skil !

Blest be thy Dew, and blest thy frost,
And happy I to be so crost,
And cur'd by Crosses at thy cost.

The Dew doth Cheer what is distrest,
The frosts ill weeds nip, and molest,
In both thou work'st unto the best.

Thus while thy sev'ral mercies plot,
And work on me now cold, now hot,
The work goes on, and slacketh not,

For as thy hand the weather steers,
So thrive I best, 'twixt joyes, and tears,
And all the year have some grean Ears.

The Pilgrimage.

As travellours when the twilight's come,
And in the sky the stars appear,
The past daies accidents do summe
With, *This wee saw there, and thus here.*

Then

Then *Jacob*-like lodge in a place
(A place, and no more, is set down,)
Where till the day restore the race
They rest and dream homes of their own.

So for this night I linger here,
And full of tossings too and fro,
Expect stil when thou wilt appear
That I may get me up, and go.

I long, and grone, and grieve for thee,
For thee my words, my tears do gush,
O that I were but where I see!
Is all the note within my Bush.

As Birds rob'd of their native wood,
Although their Diet may be fine,
Yet neither sing, nor like their food,
But with the thought of home do pine;

So do I mourn, and hang my head,
And though thou dost me fullnes give,
Yet look I for far better bread
Because by this man cannot live.

O feed me then! and since I may
Have yet more days, more nights to Count,
So strengthen me, Lord, all the way,
That I may travel to thy Mount.

Heb. Cap. xi. ver. 13.
And they Confessed, that they were strangers, and Pilgrims on the earth.

The

The Law, and the Gospel.

Lord, when thou didſt on *Sinai* pitch
And ſhine from *Paran*, when a firie Law
Pronounc'd with thunder, and thy threats did thaw
Thy Peoples hearts, when all thy weeds were rich
    And Inacceſſible for light,
      Terrour, and might,
How did poor fleſh. (which after thou didſt weare,)
      Then faint, and fear !
Thy Choſen flock, like leafs in a high wind,
Whiſper'd obedience, and their heads Inclin'd.

2.

But now ſince we to *Sion* came,
And through thy bloud thy glory ſee,
With filial Confidence we touch ev'n thee ;
And where the other mount all clad in flame,
    And threatning Clouds would not ſo much
      As 'bide the touch,
We Climb up this, and have too all the way
      Thy hand our ſtay,
Nay, thou tak'ſt ours, and (which ſul Comfort brings)
Thy Dove too bears us on her ſacred wings.

3.

Yet ſince man is a very brute
And after all thy Acts of grace doth kick,
Slighting that health thou gav'ſt, when he was ſick,
Be not diſpleas'd, If I, who have a ſute
    To thee each houre, beg at thy door
      For this one more ;
O plant in me thy *Goſpel*, and thy *Law*,
      Both *Faith*, and *Awe* ;

So

So twift them in my heart, that ever there
I may as wel as *Love*, find too thy *fear*!

4.

Let me not fpil, but drink thy bloud,
Not break thy fence, and by a black Excefs
Force down a Juft Curfe, when thy hands would blefs ;
Let me not fcatter, and defpife my food,
  Or nail thofe bleffed limbs again
   Which bore my pain ;
So Shall thy mercies flow : for while I fear,
   I know, thou'lt bear,
'But fhould thy mild Injunction nothing move me,
I would both think, and Judge I did not love thee.

John Cap. 14. ver. 15.
If ye love me, keep my Commandements.

The World.

I Saw Eternity the other night
Like a great *King* of pure and endlefs light,
  All calm, as it was bright,
And round beneath it, Time in hours, days, years
  Driv'n by the fpheres
Like a vaft fhadow mov'd, In which the world
  And all her train were hurl'd ;
The doting Lover in his queinteft ftrain
   Did their Complain,
Neer him, his Lute, his fancy, and his flights,
   Wits fo our delights ,
With gloves, and knots the filly fnares of pleafure
   Yet his dear Treafure
All fcatter'd lay, while he his eys did pour
   Upon a flowr.

         The

2.

The darksome States-man hung with weights and woe
Like a thick midnight-fog mov'd there so slow
   He did nor stay, nor go ;
Condemning thoughts (like sad Ecclipses) scowl
    Upon his soul,
And Clouds of crying witnesses without
   Pursued him with one shout.
Yet dig'd the Mole, and lest his ways be found
    Workt under ground,
Where he did Clutch his prey, but one did see
    That policie,
Churches and altars fed him, Per juries
    Were gnats and flies,
It rain'd about him bloud and tears, but he
    Drank them as free.

3.

The fearfull miser on a heap of rust
Sate pining all his life there, did scarce trust
   His own hands with the dust,
Yet would not place one peece above, but lives
    In feare of theeves.
Thousands there were as frantick as himself
    And hug'd each one his pelf,
The down-right Epicure plac'd heav'n in sense
    And scornd pretence
While others slipt into a wide Excesse
    Said little lesse ;
The weaker sort slight, triviall wares Inslave
    Who think them brave,
And poor, despised truth sate Counting by
    Their victory.

Yet

4.

Yet some, who all this while did weep and sing,
And sing, and weep, soar'd up into the *King*,
    But most would use no wing:
O fools (said I,) thus to prefer dark night
    Before true light,
To live in grots, and caves, and hate the day
    Because it shews the way,
The way which from this dead and dark abode
    Leads up to God,
A way where you might tread the Sun, and be
    More bright than he.
But as I did their madnes so discusse
    One whisper'd thus,
*This Ring the Bride-groome did for none provide
    But for his bride.*

John Cap. 2. ver. 16, 17.

All that is in the world, the lust of the flesh, the lust of the Eys, and the pride of life, is not of the father, but is of the world.

And the world passeth away, and the lusts thereof, but he that doth the will of God abideth for ever.

The Mutinie.

WEary of this same Clay, and straw, I laid
    Me down to breath, and casting in my heart
The after-burthens, and griefs yet to come,
    The heavy sum
So shook my brest, that (sick and sore dismai'd)
My thoughts, like water which some stone doth start

                Did

Did quit their troubled Channel, and retire
Unto the banks, where, storming at those bounds,
They murmur'd sore ; But I, who felt them boyl
          And knew their Coyl,
Turning to him, who made poor sand to tire
And tame proud waves, If yet these barren grounds
      And thirstie brick must be (said I)
          My taske, and Destinie,

2.

Let me so strive and struggle with thy foes
(Not thine alone, but mine too,) that when all
Their Arts and force are built unto the height
          That Babel-weight
May prove thy glory, and their shame ; so Close
And knit me to thee, That though in this vale
Of sin, and death I sojourn, yet one Eie
May look to thee, To thee the finisher
And Author of my faith ; so shew me home
          That all this fome
And frothie noise which up and down doth flie
May find no lodging in mine Eie, or Eare,
      O seal them up ! that these may flie
          Like other tempests by.

3.

Not but I know thou hast a shorter Cut
To bring me home, than through a wildernes,
A Sea, or Sands and Serpents ; Yet since thou
          (As thy words show)
Though in this desart I were wholy shut,
Canst light and lead me there with such redress
That no decay shal touch me ; O be pleas'd
To fix my steps, and whatsoever path
Thy sacred and eternal wil decreed
          For thy bruis'd reed

O give it ful obedience, that so seiz'd
Of all I have, I may nor move thy wrath
    Nor grieve thy *Dove*, but soft and mild
    Both live and die thy Child.

Revel. Cap. 2. ver. 17.

*To him that overcometh wil I give to eate of the hidden
Manna, and I wil give him a white stone, and in the stone a
new name written, which no man knoweth, saving he that
receiveth it.*

The Constellation.

FAir, order'd lights (whose motion without noise
    Resembles those true Joys
Whose spring is on that hil where you do grow
    And we here tast sometimes below.)

With what exact obedience do you move
    Now beneath, and now above,
And in your vast progressions overlook
    The darkest night, and closest nook !

Some nights I see you in the gladsome East,
    Some others neer the West,
And when I cannot see, yet do you shine
    And beat about your endles line.

Silence, and light, and watchfulnes with you
    Attend and wind the Clue,
No sleep, nor sloth assailes you, but poor man
    Still either sleeps, or slips his span.

He grops beneath here, and with restless Care
    First makes, then hugs a snare,
Adores dead dust, sets heart on Corne and grass
    But seldom doth make heav'n his glass.

Musick

Mufick and mirth (if there be mufick here)
  Take up, and tune his year,
These things are Kin to him, and muft be had,
  Who kneels, or fighs a life is mad.

Perhaps fome nights hee'l watch with you, and peep
  When it were beft to fleep,
Dares know Effects, and judge them long before,
  When th' herb he treads knows much, much more.

But feeks he your *Obedience, Order, Light,*
  Your calm and wel-train'd flight,
Where, though the glory differ in each ftar,
  Yet is there peace ftill, and no war ?

Since plac'd by him who calls you by your names
  And fixt there all your flames,
Without Command you never acted ought
  And then you in your Courfes fought.

But here Commiffion'd by a black felf-wil
  The fons the father kil,
The Children Chafe the mother, and would heal
  The wounds they give, by crying, zeale.

Then Caft her bloud, and tears upon thy book
  Where they for fafhion look,
And like that Lamb which had the Dragons voice
  Seem mild, but are known by their noife.

Thus by our lufts diforder'd into wars
  Our guides prove wandring ftars,
Which for thefe mifts, and black days were referv'd,
  What time we from our firft love fwerv'd.

Yet O for his fake who fits now by thee
  All crown'd with victory,

          So

So guide us through this Darknes, that we may
    Be more and more in love with day;

Settle, and fix our hearts, that we may move
    In order, peace, and love,
And taught obedience by thy whole Creation
    Become an humble, holy nation.

Give to thy spouse her perfect, and pure dress,
    Beauty and *holiness*,
And so repair these Rents, that men may see
    And say, *where God is, all agree.*

The Shepheards.

SWeet, harmles lives! (on whose holy leisure
    Waits Innocence and pleasure,)
Whose leaders to those pastures, and cleer springs,
    Were *Patriarchs*, Saints, and Kings,
How happend it that in the dead of night
    You only saw true light,
While *Palestine* was fast a sleep, and lay
    Without one thought of Day?
Was it because those first and blessed swains
    Were pilgrims on those plains
When they receiv'd the promise, for which now
    'Twas there first shown to you?
'Tis true, he loves that Dust whereon they go
    That serve him here below,
And therefore might for memory of those
    His love there first disclose;
But wretched *Salem* once his love, must now
    No voice, nor vision know,
        G

Her stately Piles with all their height and pride
    Now languished and died,
And *Bethlems* humble Cotts above them stept
    While all her Seers slept;
Her Cedar, firr, hew'd stones and gold were all
    Polluted through their fall,
And those once sacred mansions were now
    Meer emptiness and show,
This made the Angel call at reeds and thatch,
    Yet where the shepheards watch,
And Gods own lodging (though he could not lack,)
    To be a common *Rack* ;
No costly pride, no soft-cloath'd luxurie
    In those thin Cels could lie,
Each stirring wind and storm blew through their Cots
    Which never harbour'd plots,
Only Content, and love, and humble joys
    Lived there without all noise,
Perhaps some harmless Cares for the next day
    Did in their bosomes play,
As where to lead their sheep, what silent nook,
    What springs or shades to look,
But that was all ; And now with gladsome care
    They for the town prepare,
They leave their flock, and in a busie talk
    All towards *Bethlem* walk
To see their souls great shepheard, who was come
    To bring all straglers home,
Where now they find him out, and taught before
    That Lamb of God adore,
That Lamb whose daies great Kings and Prophets wish'd
    And long'd to see, but miss'd.
The first light they beheld was bright and gay
    And turn'd their night to day,
But to this later light they saw in him,
    Their day was dark, and dim.

Miserie.

Misery.

LOrd, bind me up, and let me lye
   A Pris'ner to my libertie,
If such a state at all can be
As an Impris'ment serving thee;
The wind, though gather'd in thy fist,
Yet doth it blow stil where it list,
And yet shouldst thou let go thy hold
Those gusts might quarrel and grow bold.
   As waters here, headlong and loose
The lower grounds stil chase, and choose,
Where spreading all the way they seek
And search out ev'ry hole, and Creek;
So my spilt thoughts winding from thee
Take the down-rode to vanitie,
Where they all stray and strive, which shal
Find out the first and steepest fal;
I cheer their flow, giving supply
To what's already grown too high,
And having thus perform'd that part
Feed on those vomits of my heart.
I break the fence my own hands made
Then lay that trespasse in the shade,
Some fig-leafs stil I do devise
As if thou hadst not ears, nor Eyes.
Excesse of friends, of words, and wine
Take up my day, while thou dost shine
All unregarded, and thy book
Hath not so much as one poor look.
If thou steal in amidst the mirth
And kindly tel me, *I am Earth*,
I shut thee out, and let that slip,
Such Musick spoils good fellowship.

G 2

Thus

Thus wretched I, and most unkind,
Exclude my dear God from my mind,
Exclude him thence, who of that Cel
Would make a Court, should he there dwel.
He goes, he yields; And troubled sore
His holy spirit grieves therefore,
The mighty God, th' eternal King
Doth grieve for Dust, and Dust doth sing.
But I go on, haste to Devest
My self of reason, till opprest
And buried in my surfeits I
Prove my own shame and miserie.
Next day I call and cry for thee
Who shouldst not then come neer to me,
But now it is thy servants pleasure
Thou must (and dost) give him his measure.
Thou dost, thou com'st, and in a showr
Of healing sweets thy self dost powr
Into my wounds, and now thy grace
(I know it wel,) fils all the place;
I sit with thee by this new light,
And for that hour th'art my delight,
No man can more the world despise
Or thy great mercies better prize.
I School my Eys, and strictly dwel
Within the Circle of my Cel
That Calm and silence are my Joys
Which to thy peace are but meer noise.
At length I feel my head to ake,
My fingers Itch, and burn to take
Some new Imployment, I begin
To swel and fome and fret within.

    " *The Age, the present times are not*
    " *To snudge in, and embrace a Cot,*
    " *Action and bloud now get the game,*
    " *Disdein treads on the peaceful name,*

" *who fits at home too bears a loade*
" *Greater than those that gad abroad.*
Thus do I make thy gifts giv'n me
The only quarrellers with thee,
I'd loose those knots thy hands did tie,
Then would go travel, fight or die.
Thousands of wild and waste Infusions
Like waves beat on my resolutions,
As flames about their fuel run
And work, and wind til all be done,
So my fierce soul bustles about
And never rests til all be out.
Thus wilded by a peevish heart
Which in thy musick bears no part
I storm at thee, calling my peace
A Lethargy, and meer disease,
Nay, those bright beams shot from thy eys
To calm me in these mutinies
I stile meer tempers, which take place
At some set times, but are thy grace,
    Such is mans life, and such is mine
The worst of men, and yet stil thine,
Stil thine thou know'st, and if not so
Then give me over to my foe.
Yet since as easie 'tis for thee
To make man good, as bid him be,
And with one glaunce (could he that gain,
To look him out of all his pain,
O send me from thy holy hil
So much of strength, as may sulfil
All thy delight (what e'r they be)
And sacred Institutes in me;
Open my rockie heart, and fil
It with obedience to thy wil,
Then seal it up, that as none see,
So none may enter there but thee.

O hear my God ! hear him, whose bloud
Speaks more and better for my good !
O let my Crie come to thy throne !
My crie not pour'd with tears alone,
(For tears alone are often foul)
But with the bloud of all my soul,
With spirit-sighs, and earneſt grones,
Faithful and moſt repenting mones,
With theſe I crie, and crying pine
Till thou both mend and make me thine.

The Sap.

COme ſapleſs Bloſſom, creep not ſtil on Earth
　　Forgetting thy firſt birth ;
'Tis not from duſt, or if ſo, why doſt thou
　　Thus cal and thirſt for dew ?
It tends not thither, if it doth, why then
　　This growth and ſtretch for heav'n ?
Thy root ſucks but diſeaſes, worms there ſeat
　　And claim it for their meat.
Who plac'd thee here, did ſomething then Infuſe
　　Which now can tel thee news.
There is beyond the Stars an' hil of myrrh
　　From which ſome drops fal here,
On it the Prince of *Salem* ſits, who deals
　　To thee thy ſecret meals,
There is thy Country, and he is the way
　　And hath withal the key.
Yet liv'd he here ſometimes, and bore for thee
　　A world of miſerie,
For thee, who in the firſt mans loyns didſt fal
　　From that hil to this vale,

　　　　　　　　　　　　　　And

And had not he so done, it is most true
    Two deaths had bin thy due;
But going hence, and knowing wel what woes
    Might his friends discompose,
To shew what strange love he had to our good
    He gave his sacred bloud
By wil our sap, and Cordial; now in this
    Lies such a heav'n of bliss,
That, who but truly tasts it, no decay
    Can touch him any way,
Such secret life, and vertue in it lies
    It wil exalt and rise
And actuate such spirits as are shed
    Or ready to be dead,
And bring new too. Get then this sap, and get
    Good store of it, but let
The vessel where you put it be for sure
    To all your pow'r most pure;
There is at all times (though shut up) in you
    A powerful, rare dew,
Which only grief and love extract; with this
    Be sure, and never miss,
To wash your vessel wel: Then humbly take
    This balm for souls that ake,
And one who drank it thus, assures that you
    Shal find a Joy so true,
Such perfect Ease, and such a lively sense
    Of grace against all sins,
That you'l Confess the Comfort such, as even
    Brings to, and comes from Heaven.

G 4   Mount

Mount of Olives.

WHen first I saw true beauty, and thy Joys
   Active as light, and calm without all noise
Shin'd on my soul, I felt through all my powr's
Such a rich air of sweets, as Evening showrs
Fand by a gentle gale Convey and breath
On some parch'd bank, crown'd with a flowrie wreath;
Odors, and Myrrh, and balm in one rich floud
O'r-ran my heart, and spirited my bloud,
My thoughts did swim in Comforts, and mine eie
Confest, *The world did only paint and lie.*
And where before I did no safe Course steer
But wander'd under tempests all the year,
Went bleak and bare in body as in mind,
And was blow'n through by ev'ry storm and wind,
I am so warm'd now by this glance on me,
That, midst all storms I feel a Ray of thee;
So have I known some beauteous *Paisage* rise
In suddain flowres and arbours to my Eies,
And in the depth and dead of winter bring
To my Cold thoughts a lively sense of spring,

  Thus fed by thee, who dost all beings nourish,
My wither'd leafs again look green and flourish,
I shine and shelter underneath thy wing
Where sick with love I strive thy name to sing,
Thy glorious name ! which grant I may so do
That these may be thy *Praise*, and my *Joy* too.

Man

Man.

WEighing the stedfastness and state
Of some mean things which here below reside,
Where birds like watchful Clocks the noiseless dare
And Intercourse of times divide,
Where Bees at night get home and hive, and flowrs
Early, aswel as late,
Rise with the Sun, and set in the same bowrs;

2.

I would (said I) my God would give
The staidness of these things to man ! for these
To his divine appointments ever cleave,
And no new business breaks their peace;
The birds nor sow, nor reap, yet sup and dine,
The flowres without clothes live,
Yet *Solomon* was never drest so fine.

3.

Man hath stil either toyes, or Care,
He hath no root, nor to one place is ty'd,
But ever restless and Irregular
About this Earth doth run and ride,
He knows he hath a home, but scarce knows where,
He sayes it is so far
That he hath quite forgot how to go there.

4. He

4.

He knocks at all doors, strays and roams,
Nay hath not so much wit as some stones have
Which in the darkest nights point to their homes,
        By some hid sense their Maker gave;
Man is the shuttle, to whose winding quest
                And passage through these looms
God order'd motion, but ordain'd no rest.

¶

I Walkt the other day (to spend my hour,)
                Into a field
Where I sometimes had seen the soil to yield
                A gallant flowre,
But Winter now had ruffled all the bowre
                And curious store
        I knew there heretofore.

2.

Yet I whose search lov'd not to peep and peer
                I'th' face of things
Thought with my self, there might be other springs
                Besides this here
Which, like cold friends, sees us but once a year,
                And so the flowre
        Might have some other bowre.

3 Then

3.

Then taking up what I could neerest spie
I digg'd about
That place where I had seen him to grow out,
And by and by
I saw the warm Recluse alone to lie
Where fresh and green
He lived of us unseen.

4.

Many a question Intricate and rare
Did I there strow,
But all I could extort was, that he now
Did there repair
Such losses as befel him in this air
And would e'r long
Come forth most fair and young.

5.

This past, I threw the Clothes quite o'r his head,
And stung with fear
Of my own frailty dropt down many a tear
upon his bed,
Then sighing whisper'd, *Happy are the dead !*
What peace doth now
Rock him asleep below ?

And

6.

And yet, how few believe such doctrine springs
From a poor root
Which all the Winter sleeps here under foot
And hath no wings
To raise it to the truth and light of things,
But is stil trod
By ev'ry wandring clod.

7.

O thou! whose spirit did at first inflame
And warm the dead,
And by a sacred Incubation fed
With life this frame
Which once had neither being, forme, nor name,
Grant I may so
Thy steps track here below,

8.

That in these Masques and shadows I may see
Thy sacred way,
And by those hid ascents climb to that day
Which breaks from thee
Who art in all things, though invisibly;
Shew me thy peace,
Thy mercy, love, and ease,

9. And

9.

And from this Care, where dreams and sorrows raign
             Lead me above
Where Light, Joy, Leisure, and true Comforts move
             Without all pain,
There, hid in thee, shew me his life again
             At whose dumbe urn
       Thus all the year I mourn.

Begging.

KIng of Mercy, King of Love,
   In whom I live, in whom I move,
Perfect what thou hast begun,
Let no night put out this Sun :
Grant I may, my chief desire !
Long for thee, to thee aspire,
Let my youth, my bloom of dayes
Be my Comfort, and thy praise,
That hereafter, when I look
O'r the sullyed, sinful book,
I may find thy hand therein
Wiping out my shame, and sin.
O it is thy only Art
To reduce a stubborn heart,
And since thine is victorie,
Strong holds should belong to thee ;

                                          Lord

Lord then take it, leave it not
Unto my dispose or lot,
But since I would not have it mine,
O my God, let it be thine !

Jude ver. 24, 25.

*Now unto him that is able to keep us from falling, and to
present us faultless before the presence of his glory with
exceding joy,*
*To the only wise God, our Saviour, be glory, and majesty,
Dominion and power, now and ever, Amen.*

FINIS.